FROM START-UP TO RAMP-UP

Indian Context and Global Insights

LEADERCREST ACADEMY

FROM START-UP TO RAMP-UP
Indian Context and Global Insights

C B Rao

LEADERCREST ACADEMY

Notion Press

Old No. 38, New No. 6
McNichols Road, Chetpet
Chennai - 600 031

First Published by Notion Press 2016
Copyright © C B Rao 2016
All Rights Reserved.

ISBN
Hardcase: 978-1-945621-81-9
Paperback: 978-1-945621-83-3

This book has been published with all efforts taken to make the material error-free after the consent of the author. However, the author and the publisher do not assume and hereby disclaim any liability to any party for any loss, damage, or disruption caused by errors or omissions, whether such errors or omissions result from negligence, accident, or any other cause.

No part of this book may be used, reproduced in any manner whatsoever without written permission from the author, except in the case of brief quotations embodied in critical articles and reviews.

DEDICATED TO

Lord Sri Venkateswara, Tirumala

Table of Contents

Introduction ix

Chapter 1
Defining Entrepreneurship 1

Chapter 2
Entrepreneurial Trinity 7

Chapter 3
Entrepreneurial Energy 15

Chapter 4
Entrepreneurial Drivers 23

Chapter 5
Transformational Entrepreneurship 31

Chapter 6
Ten Success Principles for Start-ups 43

Chapter 7
Ten Commandments of Entrepreneurship 51

Chapter 8
Technological Efficiency and Financial
Sufficiency 63

Chapter 9
Entrepreneurial Academics 73

Chapter 10
Family-Entrepreneur-Professional Triad 85

Chapter 11
Entrepreneurial Culture 95

Chapter 12
　　Financial Entrepreneurship..........................105
Chapter 13
　　National Start-up Models 123
Chapter 14
　　Entrepreneurial Ecosystems 133

Epilogue: *Entrepreneurial Thermodynamics*............... 141

About the Author and Publisher *147*

INTRODUCTION

Introduction

When a Career Journey Becomes Chapters in an Economic Continuum

It has been my fortune, over the last 42 years, to be associated with the setting up and growing up of entrepreneurial businesses, expansion and diversification of global family conglomerates, and regionalization of multinational corporations, working my way up from executive and managerial roles to leadership responsibilities as managing director and executive chairman. This journey has provided me with immensely exciting and educative opportunities to work with first generation entrepreneurs who established world-class businesses, professional business leaders with national and multinational experience, growth-oriented entrepreneurial families and innumerable brilliant minds with entrepreneurial spirit and inventive mind-set.

This unique journey has inculcated in me a deep respect for entrepreneurial way of working, and the profound impact the entrepreneurial and start-up movement can have on economic development, particularly for India now on the cusp of a new wave of growth. Entrepreneurship is quite distinct from mere management or leadership, and entrepreneurs are truly a breed apart. Start-up is even more distinctive. In their outstanding successes and disappointing setbacks, there lies a whole body of knowledge which has relevance and applicability for the theory and practice of management, and for aspirant professionals and successful leaders alike. This book on entrepreneurship is my humble effort to capture some of the nuances of entrepreneurship and bring out the challenges and opportunities for start-ups to ramp up, with Indian context and global perspectives.

This book is organised in terms of fourteen chapters, each of them dealing with a principal facet of entrepreneurship.

Introduction

Chapter 1: Defining Entrepreneurship, defines entrepreneurs and start-up founders in terms of their unique competencies and aspirations. Given that entrepreneurship is a running theme throughout the book and facets of entrepreneurship are embedded in various other chapters, the definitional chapter considers only certain critical aspects of entrepreneurship.

Chapter 2: Entrepreneurial Trinity, draws upon the Hindu analogy of the Trinity of Gods, namely Brahma, the Creator, Vishnu, the Preserver and Shiva, the Destroyer and illustrates how entrepreneurs tend to play these three roles of creation, preservation and destruction at different points of time. The chapter also brings out how entrepreneurs use forces of competence, passion and gumption to define their entrepreneurial model.

Chapter 3: Entrepreneurial Energy, discusses how energy is at the core of entrepreneurship. It propounds two paradoxes of entrepreneurship related to scale and linearity. It also discusses whether entrepreneurship tends to get stymied by limits to growth, ebbing passion or eroding energy, and proposes certain approaches for sustaining entrepreneurial energy.

Chapter 4: Entrepreneurial Drivers, specifically focuses on start-ups and observes that thematic matrix, common thread and uncommon passion are three critical drivers of most start-up entrepreneurial activity. Each of the drivers is illustrated by specific examples, with thematic matrix serving as the critical driver that provides a differentiated platform for each entrepreneurial start-up.

Chapter 5: Transformational Entrepreneurship, lays out the conceptual hues of entrepreneurship and entrepreneurs.

It traces the importance of technology, organic or inorganic, in ensuring entrepreneurial success. It explains how initial success is just one step and several entrepreneurial variations are required to ensure sustainable success. Typologies and dilemmas of entrepreneurship are an important takeaway of this chapter.

Chapter 6: Ten Success Principles for Start-ups, brings out the subtle but important differences between a start-up venture and an entrepreneurial firm. Building on that, it details ten principles for sustainable success of start-ups. It brings out how start-ups succeed by their ability to disrupt existing products and services as well as existing structures. It also cautions start-ups to avoid the pitfalls of self-disruption or competitive disruption.

Chapter 7: Ten Commandments of Entrepreneurship, focuses on the growing preference of new graduates and youngsters to take up entrepreneurship as an alternative to regular career tracks. It advises young aspirants of five features of entrepreneurship that should inspire them and five potential pitfalls that they should be wary of. Together, the ten features represent a meaningful balance for success in an Indian context.

Chapter 8: Technological Efficiency and Financial Sufficiency, discusses how technology is not only a game changer for business but also a life changer for humans. It argues that technological efficiency when supported by financial sufficiency can enable entrepreneurial firms achieve not only successful start-up but sustainable ramp-up. The chapter weaves in the concept of acquisitions capturing synergy from the combination of technological acumen of start-ups and financial sinews of large firms.

Chapter 9: Entrepreneurial Academics, discusses the importance of science and technology in ensuring a nation's economic progress and social development and the role of management and entrepreneurship in leveraging science and technology at studentship level itself to develop a unique alchemy of STEMS relevant for India in a globally competitive perspective.

Chapter 10: Family-Entrepreneurship-Professional Triad, discusses the opportunities and challenges arising out of family groups, entrepreneurial and start-up firms desiring or requiring professionals to lead their firms. It impresses upon the three stakeholders to modify their stylistic approaches to develop winning combinations and outlines how professional leaders could steer their way through the imprecision and complexities of entrepreneurial, start-up and family firms.

Chapter 11: Entrepreneurial Culture, talks of the importance of building up an entrepreneurial culture in youngsters from the student days through a mix of curricular and extracurricular activities as well as entrepreneurial pilot projects and corporate social responsibility initiatives. The need to ingrain self-reliance and entrepreneurship as a family and work ethic to shape a national entrepreneurial culture is brought out.

Chapter 12: Financial Entrepreneurship, discusses the importance of financing arrangements in supporting entrepreneurial drive. It outlines nine different but inclusive ways in which the State and Society can marshal their allocable resources to support nano, micro and small enterprises take shape and reach progressively higher levels. It hypothesizes a pivotal role for Governments to enable the various financing modes.

Introduction

Chapter 13: National Start-up Models, traces India's industrial evolution which focused on heavy industries on one hand and small scale industries on the other. It compares the US, Japanese and Indian models of start-up development, and suggests a hybrid model for Indian start-ups that leverages Indian scientific and technological institutions and which could attract investments from global venture funds.

Chapter 14: Entrepreneurial Ecosystems, develops a public policy framework that could be inspired by Japan's small and microenterprise enterprise ecosystem. Applauding the Government's move to establish MUDRA Bank, it also advocates setting up exclusive state-funded and private-participated credit enhancement and skill honing institutions.

Epilogue: Entrepreneurial Thermodynamics, marks the conclusion of the book. It offers a rather intricate engineering view of entrepreneurial systems as energy systems, following the three laws of thermodynamics on one hand and defying the laws of entropy on the other. It proposes sustainable entrepreneurial companies as fountainheads of perpetual energy.

I hope that the discussions, examples and hypotheses as well as models, constructs and formats detailed in this book bring out the fascinating hues of entrepreneurial and start-up ventures, and inspire youngsters as well as experienced professionals to join the entrepreneurship and start-up movement to create wealth for the Indian economy and society, with sustainability and equity.

C Bhaktavatsala Rao
Chennai
July 01, 2016

CHAPTER 1

Defining Entrepreneurship

Entrepreneurs: A Breed Apart?

A dictionary definition of an entrepreneur is bland and blunt: Oxford Dictionary defines an entrepreneur as a person who makes money by starting new businesses. In common business parlance, however, an entrepreneur is one who is not an employee and is more than a manager or a leader. Often, an entrepreneur starts with nothing except his or her idea or plan, hard-earned savings and, of course, passion to create a business.

There are managers and leaders who are routinely starting new businesses within companies, new companies within industries and new industries within economies. There are probably several thousands of them. What then distinguishes an entrepreneur from such managers and leaders?

An analogy would probably explain well. An entrepreneur is like a mountaineer who relies on his or her guts, energy and passion as well as a few basic tools to reach a peak. A manager or a leader is perhaps one who analyses the path and weather, and deploys a helicopter to get to the peak. There are applicable challenges and opportunities as well as costs and benefits in both the approaches.

Differentiated Icons

Not every entrepreneur is probably the same. Entrepreneurs like Henry Ford, Konosuke Matsushita, Akio Morita, Bill Gates, Steve Jobs, Larry Page, Sergey Brin and Mark Zuckerberg rewrote industrial history by creating new products or services around novel technologies, and new industries around such products or services commercialized for the first time. There were also follow-on entrepreneurs who expanded and reshaped industries or competed with the pioneers, like William Durant did with General Motors. There were entrepreneurs who created industrial history in a hostile or fledgling environment (for example, pre-independence India under British occupation) like Jamshedji Tata, Henning Holck-Larsen and Soren Kristin Toubro.

In the post-independence India, which adopted a socialistic system of governmental regulation of industrial development, entrepreneurs like Dhirubhai Ambani applied an inventive and aggressive mind to redefine what entrepreneurial initiative could deliver for business. Narayana Murthy and other co-founders of Infosys demonstrated how with little money and abundant skills one could create companies around global opportunities for India in the software industry. Dr Pratap Reddy demonstrated how a physician could transform India's healthcare scenario through his Apollo chain of corporate hospitals. First generation entrepreneurs like Raghavendra Rao of Orchid typified a whole new generation of entrepreneurial and start-up ecosystem in the post-liberalization phase with creativity, ardour and passion.

Some Questions...

Is a start-up entrepreneur an entrepreneur for life? Probably not. Somewhere along the path of growth most entrepreneurs become all too adventurous, all too confident or simply all too obsolete. Microsoft, for example, failed to see the Web revolution. Sony failed to see the flat panel revolution. Yet these firms are still surviving and growing because the entrepreneurs, in good time, created institutions with core strengths, and which as firms could reinvent themselves in the face of adversities. An entrepreneur who ceases to be a good manager or a leader (or fails to recognize the need for good management and leadership) often fails to transform his or her company into a sustainable growth engine.

Should one have limits for claiming oneself to be an entrepreneur? Probably yes. The moment an entrepreneurial venture achieves a profitable full year of operations, logically, the main defining elements of an entrepreneur (no money, no organization but only idea and passion) would have disappeared. The sooner an entrepreneur realizes that, and transforms himself into a role model of balanced leadership, the better will it be for him and his company. This is because if he is a true entrepreneur, he will look for new challenges to undertake another resource-strapped, boundary-less quest. Such a move is better for his company, because such a transformation substitutes the singular entrepreneurial zeal of the founder with the diffusion of entrepreneurial management across the company.

Is working as an entrepreneur exciting? Surely, because it is the attitude and personality that drives an entrepreneur. He or she typically likes to define his or her boundaries and rules of game. He typically works with his mind, heart and guts, simultaneously. As a result, he is able to connect logically, emotionally and inspirationally with his team members. This leads to genuineness, ownership and excitement in the team. Yet, as mentioned above, an entrepreneur needs also to know when his individual competence and satisfaction have to be subjugated to organizational capabilities and excitement.

Is it invariably exciting to work with entrepreneurs? Yes, largely because they tend to be inspirational and energetic individuals fizzing with ideas and optimism. They believe in individuals and let people experiment. Yet, in their strengths lie their own weaknesses. They fail often in drawing the line between being truly inspirational and excessively rabble-rousing. They have too many ideas to get excited about, and in trying to implement all of them they tend to cross prudential norms. Their relentless optimism sometimes strays into dangerous territory which is characterized by excessive risk-taking, a denial of reality, and persistence beyond common sense. Many successful entrepreneurs fail to delegate. Some entrepreneurs who get surrounded by incompetent individuals remind one of lessons in history where successful emperors failed to retain their successes because when they overreached they had no one around them to bring them to their senses.

All things said, entrepreneurs, including founders of start-up ventures, are the inventors, the makers and the builders of a nation's economy. Economies need them for the momentum of growth. The clever and sagacious entrepreneurs who translate their singular entrepreneurial competence into organizational capability and who surround themselves with able supporters to balance out their imperfections will make a lasting mark on the history. Throughout the following chapters, these and other definitional and executional aspects of entrepreneurship, where necessary with additional focus on specific and differentiated nature of start-ups, are brought out with contextual examples and references.

CHAPTER 2

Entrepreneurial Trinity

Three Forms of Entrepreneurs: Existential Reality or Hypothetical Paradigm?

Kishore Biyani, Founder-CEO of Future Group and a pioneer of modern retailing in India with Pantaloon, stated once that entrepreneurs are essentially of three types: the creators, the preservers and the destroyers. He said that he was a creator and a destroyer simultaneously. That Biyani has been a fantastic creator of retail format in India is well-known. Established in 1987, his Future Group operates in the Indian retail sector through over 17 million square feet of retail space, serving 300 million customers in 240 cities and 60 rural locations across the country based on products and services supplied by over 30,000 small, medium and large entrepreneurs and manufacturers from across India. Future Group employs 35,000 people directly covering every section of our society. The group revenues are variously indicated around USD 2 billion annually.

While retail forms the core business activity of Future Group, group subsidiaries are present in leisure and entertainment, brand development, retail real estate development, retail media and logistics. Some of the other businesses include, mobile telephony brand, T24, operated in association with Tata Teleservices, a supply chain and logistics infrastructure company, and a company engaged in providing educational and training services through three Future Innoversity campuses in Ahmedabad, Bangalore and Kolkata. In the financial space, Future Capital and Future Generali companies offer consumer finance and insurance to customers, as well as corporate loans and equity investments to companies engaged in consumer businesses. Where does the concept of Biyani being an entrepreneur of the destroyer type come from?

Possibly, Biyani had in mind the huge debt he had to accumulate in the aggressive attempt to build his retail, finance and services empire. This situation had led to his divestment of stake in Future Capital and parleys to unlock value from the two insurance ventures. Probably, this was also related to an effort by the group to identify core and non-core businesses. Even established companies like Ashok Leyland have faced in recent times the dilemma of core and non-core. The recent fire-sale of stressed assets by a number of high-growth entrepreneurial firms also points to the destroyer facet. This brings us to the broader question as to whether divestments by an entrepreneur are tantamount to destroying of the edifice (or parts of it) that he or she would have built with great passion. The history of mergers and acquisitions points out, on the contrary, that what appears to be destroying of the edifice ends up creating wealth for the promoters and the broader set of investors and stakeholders. This is notwithstanding the fact that in some cases divestments (and acquisitions) destroy wealth for either or both the parties.

The Theory of Trinity

The concept of the three entrepreneurial types alluded to by Biyani corresponds intriguingly and interestingly to the Hindu religious concept of the Trinity of Gods who drive the total universal and living system; Brahma, the Creator, Vishnu, the Preserver and Shiva, the Destroyer. While in the Hindu religious mythology, each of the three Gods has specific functions in the cosmic system, and rarely do they transgress the respective roles, Biyani seems to indicate that an entrepreneur could be one or more of the three roles rolled into one. It is great that entrepreneurs are playing God to the growth-dependent Indian economy; however, the concept of entrepreneurs as harbingers of change itself needs to be better appreciated by entrepreneurs and professionals to ensure that each productive activity generates value on a sustainable basis, and never destroys it.

Whether or not there indeed exist three types of entrepreneurs as postulated, entrepreneurs themselves are made up of three unique forces: competence, passion, and gumption. While without doubt, professionals also possess, and are made up of, these three attributes, these attributes are much more specific in respect of entrepreneurs. For example, an entrepreneur's competence tends to be his or her individual core knowledge that is critical to the establishment of the entrepreneurial enterprise. This is different from a professional's competence that tends to be multifarious to meet a wide range of business needs, across firms. An entrepreneur's passion is one of laying out one's own path to reach the destination of enterprise creation, often based on an intuitive call, whether others agree or not. This is different from a professional's passion that is often system compliant and duty bound. An entrepreneur's gumption is forever driven by rewards and never detracted by the risks. This is different from a professional's approach to risk-taking which is cautious and consensual.

An entrepreneur who is a creator tends to have an equal mix of competence, passion and gumption. An entrepreneur who is a preserver tends to accord greater emphasis to enterprise management by competence rather than by passion and gumption. An entrepreneur who is a destroyer believes that the limits of competence, passion and gumption have been reached. Hypothetically, an entrepreneur could be in a perpetual creator mould by entrusting preservation of enterprise to professionals, and in the process avoiding becoming a destroyer altogether. Rarely, however, businesses can sustain themselves to perpetuity independent of human errors, entrepreneurial or professional, and oblivious of environmental discontinuities, technological or competitive. An entrepreneur has to reengineer himself periodically to be able to create and preserve more and even if inevitable, destroy less.

Limits of Assumption

While the three Gods, the Creator, the Preserver and the Destroyer are the Almighty Gods, the entrepreneurs who are creators, preservers and destroyers are unfortunately not. They face an environment that supports or opposes the outcomes of creation, preservation and destroying in different ways at different points of time. Reverting to the case of Future Group, the genesis of divestment (akin to destroying of its own enterprise parts), related to its own creation, far beyond what the resources could permit or the investors could appreciate. Biyani decided to unlock value in financial sector through divestment so that the Group could defend its core of retail business in an environment that would see a massive influx of foreign direct investment. The expectation is one of further organic growth based on resources generated and/ or a partial destruction of even the core by ceding stake to a global retailer. An entrepreneur's ability or positioning to be a creator, preserver or destroyer could well depend on how the forces of environment shape to support or oppose.

A start-up entrepreneur tends to assume almost always that he or she would be a creator; for that is what entrepreneurship is all about. However, an established entrepreneur has to balance the roles of creator and preserver with dexterity so that they do not become destroyers. It is often a matter of choice for the creative entrepreneurs to hand over the reign of their successful enterprises to preservers who can sustain or grow the success. The diversified growth of entrepreneurial groups, be it Tatas or Birlas has been due to the recognition of the concept of baton change. In such scenarios, divestment or wind-down of parts of the enterprise tends to be a well-considered strategic move, rather than an entrepreneur-dependent or entrepreneur-driven action.

As a start-up enterprise, the assumptions on which an entrepreneur can operate are only a few but critical. The start-up assumption, driven by an internal core competence and an external opportunity perception, is fairly simple though intense: "I Can." However, the number of assumptions that an entrepreneur would need to manage quickly escalates as the enterprise expands, and further as enterprises become a group. The competitive forces increase in numbers and intensity as an enterprise grows in scale. It would be well-merited, even if difficult, for entrepreneurs to attempt to find out the tipping point when their own combined forces of competence, passion and gumption could be overwhelmed by the combined competitive forces of technology, market and regulation. Without sensitivity, reflection and introspection, such tipping point is rarely discovered until it is too late to find out. There is a simpler and more enduring strategy for entrepreneurs being in a perpetual mode of creation.

Reinvention

Firms, as well as their leaders, need to reinvent themselves periodically to stay contemporary and competitive.

Entrepreneurs, by definition, can neither be preservers nor destroyers; they can only be creators. Yet, it is a paradox of business history that entrepreneurs find it increasingly difficult to create new ventures once their start-up ventures become established entities. The reasons are twofold: firstly, entrepreneurs fail to recognize the competitive forces that increase rather exponentially with growth and secondly, entrepreneurs, despite growth of their enterprises, increasingly compete with professionals in the tasks of further growth or consolidation and restructuring. These two tasks are best left to professionals with requisite (not necessarily entrepreneurial level) competence, passion and gumption.

Attempts by entrepreneurs to transform themselves into preservers and destroyers would be ill-advised. In the competitive arena of business, virtually every aspect of organization and every member of organization needs periodical refreshing and retooling. Entrepreneurship is the only aspect of business that has to stay unchanged in the context of natural instincts of building start-ups, and growing them to a particular level organically, and then handing over. Entrepreneurial energy is a very unique form of energy. It should be used more for creation, leaving the tasks of preserving and destroying to professionals whose focus and energy are better suited to such tasks. The enigma of entrepreneurial energy needs to be better understood by entrepreneurs and professionals alike.

CHAPTER 3

Entrepreneurial Energy

Enigma of Entrepreneurial Energy: Paradoxes of Scale and Linearity

Given my association at senior levels with entrepreneurs and entrepreneurial organizations, I am often asked the question "who is an entrepreneur." Invariably, my answer has been that an entrepreneur is one who creates something out of nothing. I however realize fully that such a simplistic definition hardly does justice to what makes an entrepreneur and what an entrepreneur makes for the society or economy. Clearly, an entrepreneur creates wealth with his or her products and/or services that are innovative, exciting, outstanding or novel, and that are developed, manufactured or delivered. Almost invariably, this formidable activity is accomplished with very lean start-up resources, amounting to nothing more than his or her ideas and some savings. It is this unique characteristic that positions entrepreneurs in a class of their own, relative to common citizens, professional managers, governmental administrators, industrial leaders and academic scholars.

Much has been written about the skills, capabilities and attributes that characterize entrepreneurs. Two critical attributes of long standing entrepreneurs are irrepressible passion and boundless energy. Passion to achieve goals of distinction and energy that drives all actions towards the goals shape entrepreneurs into what they are. Mostly however, it is the entrepreneurial passion that is spoken of, and entrepreneurial energy rarely finds mention. If passion is the spark, energy is the fuel for entrepreneurial ventures. As automotive and chemical engineers are aware, certain fuels and chemicals can spark themselves into high energy combustion by themselves under high pressures and a spark by itself can ignite only ignitable fuels or chemicals.

Passion dims without energy, which possibly explains why entrepreneurs, as they mature, fail to translate their continued passion into sparkling ventures as they once could do.

Entrepreneurs have great expectations of themselves and their organizations. They expect their organizations to clone them in terms of passion and energy. In doing so, they ignore the differences between passion and energy on one hand, and between themselves and their organizations on the other. Passion is akin to motivation while energy is very much the motive power. It is possible for individuals to be energetic but not necessarily passionate, and *vice versa*. Passion provides the aspiration but energy leads one to achievement. Bereft of passion, sheer energy can drive results provided the entrepreneur sets a goal model. In sum, the energy quotient of the entrepreneurial system rather than its passion equation drives the growth and sustainability of an entrepreneurial organization.

Entrepreneurial Potential and Paradox

Entrepreneurship is full of potential and paradox. Nations are made competitive by entrepreneurship. New ventures are established and additional jobs are created by entrepreneurs who eschew traditional jobs and push the envelope with their passion and energy. Sunrise sectors in advanced markets and growth sectors in emerging markets offer full potential for entrepreneurial play. Product innovation, manufacturing efficiency, and delivery excellence, either singly or in combination, help an entrepreneurial venture to succeed. Clearly, in the global economic system the full entrepreneurial potential is not yet tapped because advanced countries are unable to spark entrepreneurship in mature sectors while emerging countries have no roadmap for creating crucibles of entrepreneurship in sunrise sectors. The high-cost advanced countries find it difficult to re-enact entrepreneurial play in mature and commoditized sectors while emerging markets have the potential, but not necessarily the resources, for broad based entrepreneurial play in sunrise sectors. To achieve this potential two paradoxes of entrepreneurship must be well understood and squarely addressed.

The first paradox is that entrepreneurship tends to be inversely proportional to scale. The faster and bigger an entrepreneurial enterprise becomes, the lighter its entrepreneurial passion becomes and the colder its entrepreneurial fire becomes. From Microsoft to Google, and from Sony to Ford, industrial history has several case examples of scale diluting entrepreneurship. There are several reasons for it. As entrepreneurs create industries (not merely firms!) out of their ventures they also attract follow-on entrepreneurs and competitors. As they grow organizationally, entrepreneurs integrate more managers than entrepreneurs in their organizational eco-systems and consequently become more deliberative and administrative in nature than intuitive and impulsive as they had been. Start-up entrepreneurship has more of goal directed execution and less of strategy driven execution while scale-sufficient entrepreneur firms become more process-dependent and less goal-inspired. Retaining entrepreneurial culture in an entrepreneurial firm as it grows in scale is a daunting challenge for the entrepreneur.

The second paradox is that entrepreneurship is rarely linear. If Infosys, as the information technology leader of

India, with a start-up investment of USD 10,000 in 1990 by its founders could become a USD 9.5 billion enterprise by 2016, with a net profit level of around 30 percent, cash and equivalents of 70 percent and fund raising capability of say another 5 billion, it does not mean that the firm can from now on automatically grow to a USD 100 billion enterprise by 2020. The reason is that entrepreneurial organizations as they grow become stymied by the growth boundaries of the industries and their markets. Neither arithmetic nor geometric progression in entrepreneurship would be feasible in entrepreneurial organizations unless entrepreneurs overcome the constraints of scale sensitivity outlined above and pursue out-of-the box approaches to achieve market re-growth and positional dominance. The challenge of achieving continuously exponential growth would be next to impossible, however passionate an entrepreneur is and however competent his organization is.

Limits to Growth, Ebbing Passion or Eroding Energy?

Not enough research has been conducted as to why fiery entrepreneurs who created rapid-growth organizations out of next-to-nothing resources fail to replicate their entrepreneurial magic proportionately, either in scale or scope. While the above hypotheses offer several plausible explanations, possibly there could be other reasons as well. A natural inclination to seek a better work-life balance, a satiation of capitalistic thrust that triggers entrepreneurial urge, a failure to get synergistic technology or business partners, a changing macro-economic environment or a desire to self-actualize in areas other than corporate or industrial development could be some other reasons.

Whatever be the reason, given that emerging markets are 'aspiration-driven' and 'potential-plenty,' entrepreneurs in such markets should not forget that they are instruments of national wealth creation, and the nation cannot become a superpower unless entrepreneurial fervour is personally maintained and/or is strongly institutionalized. There exist two ways to achieve this.

Entrepreneurs who are intent on retaining the individual charisma of entrepreneurship have few options other than becoming serial entrepreneurs. Successful serial entrepreneurs bring up their firms to critical scale and leave them in the hands of larger investors or partners, unlocking value and cashing out the stake, generating larger corpuses for subsequent ventures. This strategy is particularly relevant when their core entrepreneurial capabilities are not industry or technology specific or when the industry itself is on a mode of continuous expansion. India has its shining examples of serial entrepreneurs: for example, Jerry Rao, the former Citi India head who set up Mphasis and is now in the fourth act of being a champion of affordable housing, G R Gopinath who founded India's trail-blazing low cost airliner, Air Deccan and is now the creator of Deccan Express Logistics, and K Ganesh who sold his stake in his online educational venture, TutorVista, following three other exits in the past. That said, serial entrepreneurship is unlikely to be a major phenomenon in the Indian entrepreneurial scene which is marked as much by emotive attachment as by growth passion.

The second sustainable approach for institutionalizing entrepreneurial fervour lies in morphing firms into conglomerates. This unique method of institutionalization of Indian entrepreneurial spirit is best evidenced by Tata, Birla, Bajaj, Reliance, Hinduja, Essar, Dhoot, TVS, Murugappa, Apollo, and various other individual or family entrepreneurial ventures which became major conglomerates. From a simple strategic business unit (SBU) approach at the firm level to a diversified conglomerate group approach, there could be enormous opportunities for fervent entrepreneurs to co-opt other capable entrepreneurs to let them start up, and ramp up such SBUs and constituent firms as future conglomerates. Institutionalization of this approach needs a breed of professionals who are fired with entrepreneurial passion and energy as much as individual entrepreneurs are. As one dwells on this approach, it is enigmatic as to why conglomerate entrepreneurship has been a preserve of entrepreneurial families rather than individual entrepreneurs. There is a need for conceptualizing and analysing the entrepreneurial paradigm in a totally different perspective that emphasizes energy rather than passion as the key constituent.

CHAPTER 4

Entrepreneurial Drivers

Theme, Thread or Passion: What drives Successful Start-up Companies?

The start-up phenomenon is gathering pace in India. Start-up, in fact, is emerging as a concept different from entrepreneurial business. Entrepreneurship has been in existence for as long as the history of business. Trade or service, design or manufacturing, and sales or marketing, entrepreneurship has been the foundation of today's successful corporations. Entrepreneurship has been synonymous with spotting business opportunities and building a delivery infrastructure for them. Typically, an entrepreneur focuses on building a big business that can continue to thrive. All entrepreneurship is not about innovation or being the first ever to market. It is also about doing things better than others, and excelling in both well-trodden paths and in uncharted territories.

A start-up, on the other hand, is fired by an entirely different consideration. He or she seeks to convert his or her product or service idea into a technically feasible and commercially viable practical proposition. A start-up founder does not typically start off with the objective of setting up and growing a business to a certain scale and scope; his or her interest is (almost) solely on product development and proof of concept (POC). In fact, POC is the key milestone, and in some cases, even the final milestone for some start-up founders. The latter class of start-up founders would even consider selling away of their start-up companies immediately after POC as a perfectly legitimate goal. That said, risk taking and attempting something far beyond one's resources permit is a common factor between a start-up founder and an entrepreneurial founder.

Thematic Matrix

Start-ups are usually based on matrixes of certain core themes. Uber was started on a matrix of cabs and aggregation, Paperboat on a matrix of contemporary packaging and traditional Indian beverages, Lunch Box on a matrix of nutrition and delivery, TravelTriangle on a matrix of value addition and customization, Knowlarity on a matrix of voice application and cloud hosting, Bluegape on a matrix of customer idea and digital printing, Reportbee on a matrix of data analytics and performance mentoring, Grey Orange on a matrix of robotics and warehousing, Paytm on a matrix of customer loyalty and monetization, Zomato on a matrix of search and review, and so on. There are two aspects, however; almost all modern start-ups are powered by software and Internet. As with all industrial activity, one thematic start-up prompts several follow-ons.

Not all start-ups may have a unique thematic matrix but all do have a thematic matrix, for sure. Successful start-ups use thematic matrix to look at established products or services differently. Uber applied thematic matrix for something as simple as cab services while Knowlarity applied thematic matrix for modern information technology solutions. That is where start-ups score over classic entrepreneurial companies which typically look at available product-market spaces. Start-ups do not look at available product-market space for entry; rather they look at redefining or recreating the space. The intersection of the two dimensions of the thematic matrix leads to redefinition as is the case with Paperboat or Lunch Box. Certain dimensions of thematic matrixes are more universally applicable than others; for example, aggregation and analytics. So is the power of Internet and software.

Common Thread

Every individual may have skills but only a few have ideas that could utilize their skills. Even fewer have clarity as to how their ideas and skills could be dovetailed to create a product or service, and eventually a business. Those who possess the common thread of skill, idea and clarity tend to be better placed as start-up founders. There is yet another set of education, experience and experimentation forming another common thread. Typically, start-ups are co-founded by two or more entrepreneurs because multiple common threads are needed to make the product or service idea work effectively, from design to delivery. The introspective ability to identify and the intuitive ability to feel the common threads is an important component of start-up development.

Given that the actual universe that has the skills, ideas. Education and experience is large, the key to expanding and enhancing the start-up ecosystem lies in the ability to develop as many common threads as possible. The start-up system is full of examples that illustrate how start-up founders discover their common threads in successive iterations. What starts as a supply of nutritious food for school children can evolve into supply of nutritious food to elderly, and later into a comprehensive foods entity covering people across all age groups. Experience in aerospace and experience in food may combine to establish a start-up that delivers food through proprietary drones. At times, common thread need not be only between the founders or employees of a start-up. As Reportbee illustrates, teacher-student connectivity forms a common thread through evaluation as a common platform. Thematic matrix and common thread constitute the core of a start-up.

Uncommon Passion

Passion is an often misused word. Increasingly, it is being reflected to categorize individuals as leaders and followers, entrepreneurs and professionals, and so on. Passion is actually more universal in its hues. A doctor who works long hours, from early morning well into the night, to save lives is a passionate doctor. A doctor who speaks up for patient rights and clinical integrity is also a passionate doctor. So is the case with an engineer who toils to complete his design project and the one who swears by quality of design than mere timelines. In all these instances, the individuals are sacrificing something, be it family life or lucrative career. Passion, to be distinguished from hard work and diligence, faces its litmus test when it has to face the test of sacrifice. From freedom fighters to entrepreneurial icons, passionate people would typically have had periods of sacrifice. The same is the case with start-up founders who invest most, if not all, of their savings (sacrificing regular employment) in their ventures.

Co-founded start-ups rank high not only on thematic matrix and common thread but also on passion. Unlike the first two, passion is an emotional attribute influenced by both intrinsic personality and extrinsic social factors. Presence of a co-founder who can compensate for or reinforce the passion quotient certainly helps in creating successful start-ups. At the same time, founder-exits or leader-churns that happen in start-ups the moment they become successful is indicative of dilution of passion quotient and entry of familiar organizational dynamics of big corporations. It is important that founders of start-ups view passion as more than effort to successfully deliver their idea into POC; they should view it as a force that binds the organization into a hub of passion, where each supports the other, and in the overall achieves a fair work-life balance. Thematic matrix, common thread and uncommon passion (theme, thread and passion or TTP) integrate as the basic motive force of start-up success.

Idea Banking, Crowd Funding

For a thriving start-up ecosystem, a proliferation of ideas is critical. It is heartening that graduates of premier institutes are increasingly ideating during their final years and are prepared to forsake lucrative careers to pursue their ideas. Some others are shifting gears from regular employment to start-up ecosystem. Educational institutions should make idea cells as important as placement cells. Corporations should also be willing to give sabbatical to their executives to pursue their start-up ideas. Luminaries should mentor start-up projects even while they are in active service and when they are able to provide positive influence. They can pick up niches from the value chains of their businesses which can be reinforced with start-up ideas.

A review of India's successful start-ups shows that with investments ranging from a few thousands of rupees to a few lakhs of rupees, several start-ups could succeed. With angel investors and next stage investors adding their financial mite in the second and third stages, start-ups blossom as full-fledged corporations. The most difficult stage is the first stage. There are more TTP platforms waiting to become start-ups than have actually become. A liberal crowdfunding investment environment could make a significant difference to India's start-up scenario. Crowdfunding enables more differentiated start-ups to come into being as organized financing typically tends to focus on successful domains. It is also important for consultants to retool their consulting templates to chisel start-up proposals in a manner that attracts investment.

CHAPTER 5

Transformational Entrepreneurship

Transformational Entrepreneurship: First Success and Beyond

India would be a USD 10,500 billion Real GDP economy by 2035, becoming the third largest in the world in another 20 years, according to projections by Goldman Sachs. This transformation would be powered by high growth rates of around 10 percent over the next few years. Such growth would require something beyond the normal economic activity. A large burst of entrepreneurism in India would drive such an extraordinary economic transformation. Government policies and individual aspirations should therefore focus on a better understanding and execution of entrepreneurship as a driver so that the future economic potential is realized in full.

Entrepreneurship has several contextual hues, relative to the industry and the entrepreneur. The right mix of entrepreneurship would create new industries faster, and reinforce the established industries better. There may not be one best entrepreneurial type for a nation as diverse as India, and it would make sense to rank-order different entrepreneurial types in terms of relative context and potential. Such an exercise, however, would benefit from defining an entrepreneur in terms of certain basic profile. While the basic definition of an entrepreneur remains as someone who creates an enterprise out of gutsy ideas, with minimal resources and maximal passion, there are other perspectives too.

Entrepreneurial Perspectives

Besides the typical competencies, an entrepreneur can be viewed from two perspectives. The first is the attribute perspective. An entrepreneur is one who is never shy of deploying his competencies with confidence, and reinforcing them with conviction. This contrasts with the profile of a professional who could have competencies but not have the confidence to deploy them or the conviction to sustain them. A manager or leader may have access to the competencies of other professionals, and even run the enterprise; but he does it more as a call of duty, independent of his having confidence and conviction, or not. An entrepreneur, on the other hand, deploys core competencies, confidence and conviction as a combination that drives entrepreneurial passion.

The other view of entrepreneur is that he or she is a professional, manager, leader and humanist, all rolled into one. An entrepreneur, like a professional, is always ready to roll up the sleeves and put the shoulder to the wheel. From making one's own coffee to drawing one's own designs, nothing is *infra dig* for an entrepreneur. An entrepreneur is also a manager, but more so a leader. He can inspire confidence by his vision and by walking the talk. The other essential role of an entrepreneur is that of humanist. An entrepreneur needs to have a larger purpose than just making money; he needs to convince his team, especially in the start-up period that the mission he has embarked upon is of importance to quality of life for the society or the nation. Only by being a humanist can an entrepreneur integrate a larger purpose into his endeavour.

Entrepreneurial Typologies

There are also two basic entrepreneurial typologies, both of which are technology-dependent. In fact, there can be no entrepreneurship without technology. No entrepreneurial venture has ever prospered with only management, and without technology. The first type, then, is based on organic technology; technology that is developed and owned by the entrepreneur. All successful entrepreneurial ventures which became industry shaping or industry leading companies have been based on unique technologies of their founding entrepreneurs. Clearly, the greater the influx of scientists, engineers and technologists into the entrepreneurial mainstream the greater would be the value creation in the economy.

The second type is based on inorganic technology. In this model, a non-technical entrepreneur makes a collaborative deal with a technical professional or in-licenses appropriate technologies, nationally or internationally, to overcome the lack of organic technologies. Needless to say, the inorganic technology route is less certain and more expensive than the organic technology route. There are, however, circumstances when combination of organic commercial enterprise and inorganic technical expertise also makes for a winning combination. Possibly, the increasing orientation of non-technical post graduates from premier management institutes towards the techno-entrepreneurial mainstream would help the entrepreneurial movement in the country equally well.

Scoring the Initial Success

India's success with entrepreneurial efforts, especially those of first generation enterprise, has been patchy. For each successful entrepreneurial venture that made the mark in its respective global markets (for example, in pharmaceutical or jewellery space), or a few other services ventures that scored successes in the local markets (primarily in consumer goods and financial spaces), there have been several others which floundered along the way. A study of such failures indicates lack of a clear strategy and an inadequacy of execution as the two primary reasons. Strategy for an entrepreneurial company must address a clear short term market need that can be fulfilled and monetized. Long term mega strategies would fit ill in a start-up entrepreneurial format. By choosing any one of the three generic strategies of cost leadership, product differentiation and niche, but certainly not all, the entrepreneur can score the much required initial success. This strategy selection needs to be fortified with execution leadership.

Entrepreneurial ventures in Indian pharmaceutical space, for example, succeeded by focusing on the niche format from the inception; a niche of relative exclusivity in product space, and a clear understanding of the drivers for such exclusivity such as technology, quality, investment, global orientation and people. Once the initial success was achieved, such pharmaceutical companies were able not only to replicate and extend the niche strategy but also experiment with product diversification, with more investible resources and cost leadership becoming available to drive scale. At the same time, a few entrepreneurial companies in the pharmaceutical field and BPO space failed to consolidate their early gains because of an attempt to follow a medley of strategies, made worse by indifferent execution, from the beginning. Initial success of entrepreneurship, therefore, needs a carefully calibrated strategy, that balances growth and profitability, for sustainability.

Beyond the First Success

While the first success is in itself a formidable challenge, growing beyond the first success is a greater challenge for the entrepreneur. For the new generation Indian economy, past entrepreneurial success is no indicator for future entrepreneurial path. This is majorly because of the structural changes that are taking place in the Indian and global economies. The new Indian economy is not merely one of cost leadership, import substitution or export competitiveness. Not many, for example, predicted even a couple of years ago that there would be a larger number of smart phone introductions than low cost phones each year or that mobile phones would ever be manufactured in India. These and several other high end products offer enormous potential to develop high technology hardware and software for the new generation of techno-commercial entrepreneurs. At the same time, there are areas of the economy which are crying for attention such as genuine micro finance, low income health solutions, universal primary education, healthy packaged food, drinking water and sanitation, nutrition and multimedia in education and so on which make a perfect canvas for the new breed of techno-savvy social entrepreneurs.

Entrepreneurs seeking fresh successes beyond the first success need not, and should not, repeat or replicate the past models that were operationally relevant in the old Indian economy. Even if necessary, entrepreneurs should be prepared for changing their canvas after the initial success and adopting a different strategic direction. Many successful entrepreneurs baulk at that challenge; strange as it may seem many entrepreneurs are not keen to restart their entrepreneurial journey from a zero base, albeit in a different field, after the first success. Several successful entrepreneurs would prefer to build future successes on their first successes, and what is worse, in the same but obsolete entrepreneurial format. While replication of a previously successful format may not appear to be an incorrect strategy (akin to sticking to core competencies), and has some economic logic, entrepreneurs also must realize that they would be missing on great new opportunities due to their diffidence to reinvent themselves.

Dilemmas of Entrepreneurship

Transformational entrepreneurship is easier aspired for than actually achieved. Entrepreneurs typically face dilemmas on paths to follow after the first success, each with its pros and cons. There are at least four ways the paths can be deciphered. Entrepreneurs can be 'stay-on' or 'move-on' entrepreneurs; they can also be 'deep divers' or 'wave surfers.' In their approaches they can be either scalar or vector. They can be serial entrepreneurs or stable entrepreneurs. They can be industry specialists or conglomerate seekers. The unique and distinctive entrepreneurs in the entrepreneurial class would have a mix of all these approaches. Transformational entrepreneurship indeed requires much more creativity, effort, diligence and effort than the first entrepreneurial venture.

Stay-on entrepreneurs stay committed to being entrepreneurial in thinking all through their life. Move-on entrepreneurs view their being entrepreneurial merely as a transitory phase in life. While initial or subsequent failures could make some entrepreneurs move-on entrepreneurs, whether being a stay-on or move-on entrepreneur has to do more with the combination of competencies, confidence, conviction and passion that one possesses as alluded to earlier. Typically, stay-on entrepreneurs tend to be not only more tenacious in their entrepreneurial mission and more successful in their first ventures but also have an enabling family environment that has greater sustainability in the face of entrepreneurial risks.

Deep-dive entrepreneurs are those who challenge the classic limits on industry definition. An entrepreneur manufacturing alternators, for example, would not see the product as only one entrepreneurial opportunity; rather he would see each sub-component, be it the shell, the wiring, the contact points, or the electronics of the alternator, as an entrepreneurial opportunity providing value enhancing scope for business expansion. Typically, such entrepreneurs utilize points of inflection in product and process technologies to deepen their understanding of new entrepreneurial opportunities. The wave-surf entrepreneurs, on the other hand, adopt a different approach of broader coverage. The manufacturer of alternators, for example, would move on to other electrical and electronics systems, and would avoid deeper integration into any one product.

Scalar entrepreneurs are typically scale driven. Vector entrepreneurs are conscious of the direction they take as well as the scale they reach. Scalar entrepreneurs tend to take on any opportunity as long as it provides scale; emphasis tends to be on magnitude rather than on a cohesive thread of strategy. The approach of Sahara group to take on anything from airlines and media houses to townships and consumer products on a grand scale is an example. In one way, scalar entrepreneurs tend to develop conglomerates randomly, with high risk, associated also with a need to exit some. Vector entrepreneurs are clear that scale needs to be sensible from the point of view of product, process or customer. Sahara group's exit from airlines business and Jet group's acquisition of Sahara Airlines brings out the scalar-vector differentiation clearly.

Serial entrepreneurs are classic wealth creators, usually for themselves, with no emotional attachment to their ventures or domains. A typically modern Western phenomenon, serial entrepreneurship has started influencing the Indian entrepreneurial psyche too. True serial entrepreneurship is based on the premise that a venture that has been successful up to a particular level in the hands of an entrepreneur would be more competent in the hands of a larger player who can take it to full potential. Serial entrepreneurship which is based on opportunistic exit as in the case of Ranbaxy in India shakes the investor and employee confidence in the long term sustainability of vector entrepreneurship in an emerging economy. Stable entrepreneurs, on the other hand, tend to be vector entrepreneurs driving logical integration or related diversification through measured steps.

Domain entrepreneurs are the most common breed of entrepreneurs. They stand specialized in their chosen starting field and build scale and scope in that field despite the several other domains that may emerge from time to time. The growth of such enterprises therefore tends to be economy or market linked. The domain entrepreneurs need to be technologically savvy to survive and grow. Conglomerate entrepreneurs, on the other hand, pursue a deliberate strategy of entry into each domain that opens up with the times and growth of economy. In the past, conglomerate entrepreneurs in India tended to move into all the licensed domains as they came to be opened up, and thus register success after success. With only a few domains remaining to be opened up, today's conglomerate entrepreneurs would need to possess better capabilities to identify technological and market opportunities.

'Mix and Grow' Entrepreneurship

Given that entrepreneurship is in itself an artful science of coping with uncertainty, it would be inappropriate to postulate that any particular model or combination of models would drive India's economic transformation. Clearly, however, no single model of entrepreneurship helps entrepreneurs post sustained successes beyond the first success. The most successful model could be to become a vector entrepreneur in a chosen field, and build scale and scope with the help of entrepreneurially oriented professional managers. The entrepreneurs should then ideally move on to new fields of diversification, replicating in each field the vector entrepreneurial strategy. This is the model successfully established by India's major entrepreneurial groups such as Tata, Birla, Murugappa and Ambani groups. In contrast, entrepreneurs such as Bajaj chose to stay focused as domain specific vector entrepreneurs. The mix of domain-vector and conglomerate entrepreneurial strategies, however, provides the maximum potential for larger market presence, faster growth and more dominant contribution to the larger society.

The ability of an entrepreneur to adopt the vector-conglomerate model clearly depends on the entrepreneurialism that he is able to develop in his professional team. Vertical integration in the vector entrepreneurial phase and related or unrelated diversification in the conglomerate entrepreneurial phase are proportionate to the entrepreneurial energy of professionals. Each Tata group company, for example, has had at least five to ten senior leaders with demonstrated capability and track record in taking entrepreneurial decisions for new products and new facilities or acquisitions. The stay-on entrepreneur should, as part of the first success, develop his leaders as professional entrepreneurs with the space to take decisions on new businesses. Similarly, success in the conglomerate phase would depend on the ability to co-opt proven entrepreneurial leaders. Successes of both the Reliance groups (Mukesh and Anil) in conglomerate diversification in new fields such as petro-chemicals, oil refining, oil and gas exploration, telecom services, power, infrastructure, media, financial services and retail space are as much due to the Ambani brothers' reinventing their entrepreneurial energies as due to their successes in getting the right kind of entrepreneurial leaders. More Indian entrepreneurs need to take note of these successful approaches to help India become the third largest economic power by 2035 as forecast.

CHAPTER 6

Ten Success Principles for Start-ups

A Theory of Successful Start-ups: Ten Principles of Sustainable Success

Entrepreneurial ventures have always been the core of new business generation, and the most visible form of not only self-employment but also generating employment for scores of people. However, over the last few years, the word 'start-up' has been in increasing circulation in business and social media. The current and future times clearly belong to start-up as the more profound form of entrepreneurship. Strictly from a dictionary point of view, a start-up company or a start-up is an entrepreneurial venture or a new business in the form of a company, partnership or temporary organization designed to search for a scalable and repeatable business model. This definition hardly brings out the distinctive or differentiating colour of start-ups. A more practical and true-to-the-ground definition of start-up provides a different and relevant perspective.

From a real life point of view, a start-up is a company working to solve a problem where the solution is not obvious and success is not guaranteed. This is the fundamental characteristic of a start-up, as differentiated from any other venture that may be established by normal entrepreneurs or existing companies. An example or two would make the concept clear. The concept of exclusive retirement homes for senior citizens, usually located in outer suburbs as gated communities, is gaining ground. An entrepreneur may set up such a project in a new city or in the same city in a different format. A start-up, however, would try to find a way in which such senior citizen services could be offered in the current mixed neighbourhoods, without moving senior citizens out of their current homes. The former, while it has its entrepreneurial risk, largely works on a proven business model. The latter, a true start-up, seeks to create a new business model out of the idea of serving senior citizens creatively.

More Fuzzy, More Valued

Start-ups usually have a fuzzy or unclear texture. One can certainly make out the shape of a fuzzy object but would find the edges hard to describe. A start-up is also like that; it is indeed easy to synchronize with the start-up idea but difficult to understand the details. It is this fuzziness that makes start-ups attractive for investors looking for the next breakthrough business opportunity to cash in on. In fact, the more novel a start-up is the more attractive the valuation could be, provided that the fundamental basis of the idea has been validated in a pilot. Another example could make things clearer. Providing microfinance to the underprivileged is by now a proven concept. However, providing microfinance exclusively for drinking water and sanitation purposes could be an idea that connects current governmental missions with focussed needs of rural population in India. The concept could be understandable but the business model by which the concept would be workable and viable is fuzzy.

The skill and passion as well as the diligence and determination of a start-up founder make such fuzzy ideas work. To be realistic, while they may work in most cases, they could also fail in certain cases. Once the fuzzy idea is workable the market opportunity could be enormous. Unlike an entrepreneurial venture which relies on a superior competitive strategy or execution, the start-up once successful as an idea writes its own rules and develops its own industry structure. The incentives to investors and employees, in a successful start-up, are therefore more exciting compared to a normal entrepreneurial venture. The incentives are compounded because a start-up tends to pass on its ownership from time to time based on increasing investment requirements for scaling up on one hand and investor appetite opening up cash-out opportunities for founders and employees (who have been issued stock options) on the other hand.

Ten Sustainable Principles

While the theory of successful start-ups is, no doubt, exciting there tends to be many a slip between the cup and the lip. The margin for error in a start-up is low while the temptation to err is high. Ten principles which could help start-ups be successful, and in a sustainable manner, are detailed below.

Ideas from environment

Start-ups do not necessarily require fundamental product discoveries or process innovations. Start-ups, however, surely require an inventive mind to understand the latent needs of socio-economic environment and provide creative products and services. This has been accomplished through either digital aggregation or disintermediation until recently but could entail artificial intelligence and internet of things in future. Start-ups succeed when they understand creative use of new technologies.

Strength through partnership

Start-ups are usually based on certain singular ideas and unique core competencies of their founders. Competencies are, no doubt, critical in converting ideas into reality. However, converting an inventive idea into a successful business requires more than technical competence, organization building or external interface, for example. Co-founders who work together, share and synergize responsibilities have tasted higher levels of success.

Differentiated employees

Just as founders of start-ups are different, employees of start-ups are also different. They are not solely motivated by monthly salaries or career progressions as understood in large organizations. They are also willing to commit their efforts and time in advance to see the success of the start-up ideas. Heart of heart, some of them could be nurturing the idea of becoming founders of future start-ups too. Selection of the first employees for a start-up with this zeal for the future, rather than with a comfort for the past, is important to create the right start-up culture in the organization.

Funding needs to be humbling

The high point of start-up ecosystem is the excitement of exponentially escalating serial funding. Responsible start-ups view such funding as a humbling reminder and positive reinforcement of their commitment to ideas, investors and consumers. There are, however, some not so responsible start-ups which, carried away by such funding, expand operations adventurously; some even splurge irresponsibly. Such start-ups fold up sooner than later. Recent experience suggests that 'down-rounds' (current valuations being lower than earlier valuations) would increase if spending out of funding is not prudent.

Capitalism through socialism

Start-up is, in essence, capitalism in an intellectual form. The objective of making money is certainly a visible trigger for all start-ups. However, they also need to have a socialistic fabric in that founders and employees should be willing to put their ideas, efforts and time together to work in advance with low remuneration, and be willing to wait for future wealth. The system encourages sharing of wealth (or, the plain of lack of it) until at least a particular stage is reached. Some start-up founders also live a relatively Spartan life as their co-founders or their employees live. Although the start-up system is capitalistic, the pathway is a trifle socialistic; to that extent it is appropriate for emerging economies such as India.

More sunrises than sunsets

Start-up ecosystem is inherently optimistic. It tends to take failures in its stride and move on. Established businesses are influenced by analytical data of successes and failures at an industry level while start-ups believe in the success potential of their ideas rather than the failures encountered by their peers. What is unique is that entry into the start-up ecosystem is not governed by conventional strategic analysis of entry and exit barriers. It would, therefore, be somewhat antithetical for a start-up to work on a business plan of classical mode; rather it needs a business plan that is idea-execution centric, with no frills.

Sustainability, rather than shareholding

The mind-sets of start-up founders tend to be somewhat paradoxical; they are at one level extremely passionate about their creative ideas but at the same time they are willing to let go of their firms if sustainability is better assured in more endowed and more powerful hands. While cashing out is no doubt a driver, start-ups have a more practical, and if one may say so wiser, approach to sustainability than typical large scale entrepreneurs. The ability of a start-up founder to manage the paradox is a vital ingredient.

Self-promotion is vital

Self-promotion is often seen as a narcissistic trend in structured organizations, and even from the perspective of a broader social interface. For a start-up, however, self-promotion is critical as usually there is none other than the start-up founder who believes in the story of the start-up. An ability to conceptualize and articulate the start-up value proposition and the competencies of the founders is an essential requirement for start-up success. If a start-up founder is introvert and unlikely to enjoy such self-promotion, partnership with a co-founder who is an extrovert and a persuasive communicator could be a way of overcoming the limitation.

A sense of urgency

Start-ups, unlike more structured entrepreneurial ventures, do not have all the time in the world to bring their ideas to fruition. Cash burnout is one issue in the initial stages; and even after the first success the need to generate surplus cash is another. In a market waiting for ideas, if an idea takes time to become feasible and commercial, there could be superior ideas floating in with superior execution. A sense of urgency is vital; however, it is not to be confused with a sense of recklessness or doing things without thinking through.

Serialization

A start-up is never a start-up for ever; it fades or blooms. Successful start-ups which stay on have a responsibility to steer themselves seamlessly into a structured corporation. Those who cash out have an even more primal responsibility to keep utilizing their core competences to establish new start-ups serially. In both the cases, managements have a responsibility to encourage start-ups in domains or activities that can be outsourced.

Disruption but not self-disruption

One of the important factors for start-up success is their ability to disrupt existing products and services as well as industry structures. In this quest, start-ups also go in for maverick leaders and leadership styles. The urge to be different and disruptive should not be allowed to result in self-disruption. There are unfortunately many examples of brilliant ideas and emerging models getting derailed by disruption. A positive mix of the above ten principles could be a robust insurance against such trends.

Start-ups also must be cognizant of the fact that disruption could be a competitive tool in the hands of other competitors, start-up or established. Although not comparable, the manner in which tablets have disrupted the laptop market but are now finding potential disruption from convertibles illustrates that disruption is a good entry strategy for a start-up but such a start-up also needs to guard against complacency, and in fact develop competitive shields to protect itself through the proof-of-concept and growth phases.

CHAPTER 7

Ten Commandments of Entrepreneurship

Ten Commandments of Indian Entrepreneurship: Five Inspirational and Five Precautionary!

There were times when graduates of premium engineering and management institutes never thought of anything other than professional corporate career as an alternate employment option. Things have changed significantly in current times with young professionals forsaking attractive employment offers and going in for entrepreneurial ventures. There was, of course, the more established trend of moving into entrepreneurship after a few years of work experience and accrual of savings. Both segments reflected first generation entrepreneurship. India Bulls, Bharti, Apollo, Orchid, Sun, RedBus, Wellspun, Dusters, JustDial, Flipkart and a host of entrepreneurial companies are examples of such entrepreneurial initiatives. Within the first generation entrepreneurship, the class that jumps into the entrepreneurial journey straight after education needs special kudos. They may be called India's new age entrepreneurs. While business management and leadership are common across all enterprises, established or entrepreneurial, there are certain guidelines which Indian entrepreneurs must be cognizant of to a greater extent.

Young entrepreneurs are usually full of academic accomplishment and growth aspiration, and typically imbue their immediate environment with high energy and anticipatory excitement. They also tend to act with the guts that are required to turn their dreams into realities. While it is difficult to hypothesize when and how young graduates are influenced in favour of entrepreneurship, the placement season, more often than not, tends to be the period when they get to know not only their worth but also whether their aspirations and corporate offerings match. The placement season is not only a time of futuristic direction and career shaping but also a period of self-awareness. That is the period when all students feel equipped to enter industry or business, but some feel inspired to give back to the society in terms of wealth creation through organizations and businesses they aspire to establish. As youngsters aspire to become entrepreneurs, here are ten principles which are particularly relevant for successful and sustainable entrepreneurship.

The Context

Most young entrepreneurs get their entrepreneurial call as they pursue management programs. The reasons are not far to seek. Management programs, in particular, provide students with a unique value addition that puts the basic academic capabilities, be it engineering, science or commerce, to even more efficient and effective use. Management programs equip a graduate with unique conceptual and analytical skills which help one view complex business problems in terms of their simple core issues on one hand and at the same time splice them in terms of diverse perspectives with insightful analytics on the other. In addition, the programs equip people with multiple soft skills, the main skill being people skills. The institutes and programs prepare the students not merely to be managers of day-to-day operations but also be equipped to become potential leaders who can shape the strategic future of organizations.

That said, there is a valid concern that scientists and technologists would be straying away from their core if they pursue management programs. The only way this concern can be mitigated is through letting the managerial thinking create the spark of entrepreneurship. India holds great potential; all economists agree that India would be the third largest economy of the world by around 2035. Statistics, however, tell only one part of the story. In qualitative terms, India's growth has been more in terms of islands of manufacturing excellence, retail luxury or social affluence. India needs to do much more in terms of social infrastructure, be it schools, colleges, universities, hospitals or industrial infrastructure, be it power, roadways, railways, seaports and airports. The opportunity for multiple contributions by young professional aspirants to Indian economy therefore stands out, the opportunity is not merely one of a regular job rather it is more of making a difference through an entrepreneurial spirit, of creating wealth and jobs for the nation, and of improving the quality of life across all sections of the society.

The Challenge

The journey as an entrepreneur is not only the most challenging but also the most satisfying one. The journey is challenging because, more often than not, an entrepreneur would have nothing but his or her dream to pursue and convert into reality. The entrepreneur is most likely to lack the organization, the financial resources, and in some cases even the emotional support of his or her near and dear as he or she pursues the entrepreneurial journey. That said, it is this challenge of creating something valuable from almost nothing, against all odds, in pursuance of one's dream makes for the entrepreneurial excitement. No entrepreneurial journey, however, cannot commence without seed capital to support the dream idea. The more fortunate ones step up from the initial security of their regular self-employed businesses, for example pharmaceutical distribution or medical practice, to venture into product development and manufacture or healthcare service; Sun Pharma's Dilip Sanghvi and Apollo's Dr Pratap Reddy, respectively, are two examples. Many others leverage their professional employment opportunities, in India or abroad, to generate savings.

Either way, one would have to go through the tribulations and excitement of an entrepreneurial journey. Even the most successful entrepreneurial behemoth cannot be immune to vicissitudes. Dr Reddy's, which seemed to make no wrong move in its scale-up journey, hit a bad patch subsequent to the acquisition of Betapharm in Germany. To be a successful entrepreneur, one may hypothesize a three step process. The first is self-discovery; a recognition of the yearning within to be an entrepreneur. The second is the ability to spot a niche. The third is the ability to raise the required seed capital. The ecosystem for entrepreneurs in India pales in comparison to the one that exists in the USA. It is to the credit of the new age entrepreneurs that they are undaunted. For example, Ola, a taxi service start-up founded by two IIT-Bombay graduates has succeeded in starting its services and raising funds ahead of global giant like Uber making an entry into India. So do the likes of Café Coffee Day in being ahead of Starbucks in India, for example. Whether it is lateral entrepreneurship or new age entrepreneurship, there exist certain commandments; by recognizing them, entrepreneurs can institutionalize growth and sustainability in their entrepreneurial ventures.

High Fives

First and foremost is the discovery of the intrinsic inspiration and passion within a person to become an entrepreneur. All successful entrepreneurs (and even unsuccessful ones) would agree that there could be no avocation more challenging and exciting than that of being an entrepreneur. The satisfaction of creating a business of value to the society, of building an organization creating employment, and developing a brand that brings recognition to the nation are well worth all the problems one would face in assembling a likeminded team, finding progressive investors and creating an R&D, manufacturing and marketing infrastructure. Dedication and commitment of an authentic entrepreneur would be such that even if he or she were given an option to restart life after a degree, he or she would unhesitatingly choose to be an entrepreneur again.

Secondly, and this is as important to established businesses as to entrepreneurial start-ups, the right business choice is one which helps an entrepreneur secure a toehold. Within any business, product choice is what makes or breaks a business; a right product choice, backed by the deployment of efficient process technology, provides sustainability to business. The success of new age entrepreneurs lies in reinventing ordinary services into new customer-centric services deploying new technologies of development, manufacture and delivery. Even ordinary businesses like recruitment, coffee serving, cloth washing and ticket booking can be viable entrepreneurial activities with a dash of technology and a feel of customer-fulfilment, achieving differentiation and sustainability in the process.

Thirdly, nimble execution is as critical as differentiated strategy, especially to entrepreneurial firms. Execution cannot be at the cost of quality though. Ability to establish a quick but perfect beachhead not only optimizes the investment-revenue equation but also raises entry barriers to all others. Many successful real estate firms began their journey by delivering their first projects fast and perfect. Great Lakes Institute of Management in Chennai, set up by Professor Bala Balachandran, has to its credit the fastest execution time frame for a high quality academic infrastructure of its kind. Establishing or accessing world-class R&D and manufacturing infrastructure in record time frames, developing products and securing regulatory approvals in the shortest time frame is a sure prescription for success in the scale-up phase of an entrepreneurial start-up.

Fourthly, sustainable competitive advantage is derived by operating at opposite ends of spectrum without compromise to any one factor; for example, being the highest quality producer with the lowest cost position, being lean in organization but powerful in delivery, harmonizing the simplicity of design standardization with customer desires for product variety, balancing efficiency requirements of high throughput with market needs of low batch sizes, and last but not the least driving high revenue and market share without compromise to profitability and sustainability. It is important for entrepreneurs to focus on the critical parameter that differentiates one's competitiveness and then reinforce it. An ice cream maker, for example, has to focus on two essential parameters: access to high quality milk and integration of a cold chain. Everything else, comes next.

Fifthly, technology ought to play a major role in whatever entrepreneurs conceive of, and execute. If Flipkart, despite being a first generation enterprise, could secure a leading position in the highly competitive e-retailing format, it is in no small measure due to its unswerving emphasis on high technology, including certain quality and compliance differentiators specific to Indian e-purchase environment. Entrepreneurs often are forced to make choices between technological competitiveness and resource optimization. Those who persevere with technology eventually end up successful. The case of MTR Foods in terms of newer technologies driving value despite the limitations of a family enterprise is an example.

Check Fives

While the above are significant positive principles for a successful entrepreneurial journey, there also exist some pitfalls one must be aware of. Firstly, as a first generation enterprise, it is an eternal struggle to overcome the limitations of financial resources. Given the classic preference in the Indian stock markets that promoter should stay invested in the company with high promoter share-holding, it is a challenge to raise risk capital through stock exchanges without dilution. Perforce, one is required to depend on debt. The race to become what one is capable of in terms of product, manufacturing and marketing canvas has to be tempered by prudential norms of debt-equity structure from time to time. Dilution of equity and monetization of non-core assets would become inevitable, to restore balance sheet stability and sustain future growth, however emotionally painful such options would seem to be.

Secondly, as a company evolves from being an entrepreneurial start-up to become a more organized enterprise it is important to keep developing organization structures and talent profiles as well as systems and processes that move in step with changing business requirements. The art of management and leadership varies significantly between a start-up and an established enterprise; the leadership teams must display a high degree of self-awareness and sensitivity in this important aspect. Even a highly successful company such as Infosys struggled with the challenge of reinventing itself to meet the increasing competition in the technology industry and the increasing aspirations of leaders for positions of influence and power.

Thirdly, all organized activity, including its competitive advantage, will stem from people, and only people. The success of a first generation enterprise such as Orchid Pharma in becoming a globally recognized pharmaceutical major had been directly linked to the founder's ability to attract stalwarts in science, engineering and business to his firm, and leverage their competencies to achieve aggressive technological development and business growth. The real source of competitive advantage of an entrepreneurial firm would lie in its ability to attract the best talent with inspirational goals and empowering ecosystem. The day a front ranking organization loses the ability to attract and retain such talent, one may say that the organization has lost its soul!

Fourthly, as entrepreneurs scale up their organizations and businesses, they must learn to evolve from the science of making right product choices to the art of making right business choices. As a successful entrepreneur, once he or she brings up a business to a critical mass, he or she must learn how to forego control, entrust it to other professionals and redirect his or her entrepreneurial entry and passion into newer vistas of growth. Inability to make this transition in a timely and graceful manner could cost the entrepreneur's business dearly and also sub-optimize future potential immensely. The split announced by Indiabulls' three promoters indicates their realization that their business had outgrown their desire to stay together.

Fifthly, entrepreneurs, at least the successful ones, would need to look beyond their own firms and businesses, and consider how they can contribute to creation of virtuous ecosystems in the country that institutionalize entrepreneurial spirit. This requires establishment of a positive climate of angel investing, start-up investment and equity investment besides an institutional framework for incubation of ideas. This requires that entrepreneurs should not be lost in the success of their enterprises but must interact with the broader stakeholder community so that India can be truly a nation of entrepreneurs. While N R Narayana Murthy's private venture fund Catamaran is an example, various other hugely successful entrepreneurs and entrepreneurial groups can do much more, if they put their heart to creating an Indian entrepreneurial ecosystem.

Ten Commandments

The growth of India's private sector has been that of India's entrepreneurship, right from the historical days of Tatas and Birlas. Indian entrepreneurship has been less flamboyant than it ought to have been, given its successes.

The potential to maximize new age entrepreneurship is also less recognized than it ought to be. India's future still has several challenges of scarcity and inequity, but with dedicated and diversified entrepreneurship each challenge is an opportunity of development for both established businesses and entrepreneurial start-ups. As one embarks upon an entrepreneurial journey, the ten themes of entrepreneurship, five inspirational and five precautionary, discussed in this chapter, should be of inspiration and guidance.

CHAPTER 8

Technological Efficiency and Financial Sufficiency

Technological Efficiency + Financial Sufficiency = Sustainable Growth: The Winning Formula for Corporate Sustainability

June 2016 saw a bold move by Microsoft, the software giant, to acquire LinkedIn, the business and professional networking firm, and once an entrepreneurial start-up, for an impressive valuation of USD 26 billion. Microsoft and LinkedIn stated that the acquisition would serve futuristic business, office and professional productivity considerations immensely well. This networking acquisition follows the path-breaking deal of February 2014 that enabled Facebook acquire WhatsApp, the highly popular social networking firm. That WhatsApp, a technology start-up, which achieved a user base of 450 million through its private messenger service in just three years from inception, could garner a deal value of USD 19 billion was certainly amazing at that time. Yet, Mark Zuckerberg, the Founder-CEO of Facebook went on record to say that WhatsApp was worth much more (a fact now borne out by the fact that the user base crossed one billion over the next two years!). The acquisition was a considered attempt by Facebook to stay relevant to the younger generation which started becoming less infatuated with Facebook in part, and began getting increasingly attracted by the exclusivity, privacy and snappiness of WhatsApp. While the Facebook - WhatsApp deal has attracted huge interest, one cannot overlook certain other technology deals of the past with similar eye-popping nature of their times. The deals, in fact, are indicative of an interesting dimension of the technology behemoths – despite their rapidly ramped up scales and large market capitalizations they remain respectful of the value technologically savvy start-ups can bring to the future businesses.

The more prominent of the past technology deal history has been the Google - YouTube deal. When Google acquired YouTube in October 2006 at a deal value of USD 1.65 billion, many thought that it was a risky foray by Google into a disorganized and often self-compelling online video streaming service. Yet, YouTube has emerged to be one of the most successful technology acquisitions ever, and probably the most notable amongst all of Google products, aside of the core Google search engine product. Equally important has been Google's acquisition of the Android mobile operating system start-up in August 2005 for an undisclosed sum. Android has since raced, under Google, to become the most dominant mobile operating system, overtaking iOS of Apple. Other notable deals are Microsoft - Hotmail (December 1997, USD 500 million), Microsoft - Skype (May 2011, USD 8.5 billion), Google - Instagram (April 2012, USD 1 billion) and Yahoo - Tumblr (August 2013, USD 1.1 billion) acquisitions, each with its compelling logic. These deals, which are only a few of the several scores of the deals that have happened, and which will no doubt be followed by several others of such unique nature, signify certain important lessons for corporate growth and sustainability.

Technology Bets as Game Changers

Many of such amazing acquisitions are seen to be bets placed by the acquirers on promising start-up technologies and rapidly revving up businesses. When such technologies succeed in shaping new user functionalities and behaviours, more especially and more strongly under financially stronger acquirers, they become truly game changing, both as technologies themselves, and as drivers for the acquirers' businesses. While such acquisitions seem to be technology bets, they actually signify a wise appreciation by the larger acquiring firms of the futility of trying to organically emulate the successful start-ups against a background of the need for such new technological functionalities. The time-point when a technology ceases to be a futuristic bet and instead becomes a business booster is a case by case occurrence.

From a strategy perspective, acquisition of such promising niche technologies and businesses is validated by the superior performance of such acquired entities and acquiring firms, post such acquisitions. All these acquisitions point to bets on novel technologies becoming game changers for businesses. Some of these have been huge bets in a technical sense (technology was not yet proven but the acquirer placed the bet with financial ease) while some have been huge bets in a financial sense (technology was well proven but the acquirer placed rather high financial bid). In the former category we have Google's acquisition of an unproven Android at a relatively low price while in the latter case we have Facebook's acquisition of WhatsApp and Microsoft's acquisition of LinkedIn at very hefty price tags. It is also interesting that in most cases, the branding of the acquired entities continued to be maintained indicating that niche technologies have their own market following and brand equity.

Breakthrough Ideas are Non-linear

Conventional strategies tend to be anchored around linear development of technologies and businesses. For example, if email was successful in the 1990s as a popular niche technology of instant communication, all subsequent efforts focused on making the email more powerful and more collaborative, for example an Outlook version. If Facebook wove an expanding open social community, Google+ attempted to build multiple circles of communities. Successful technologies tend to be non-linear, however. Twitter achieved success with the instantaneous brevity of 140 character messaging. WhatsApp achieved success through texting service that is both free and private, extending equally well on audio and video channels as well as Internet telephony later on, and with end-to-end fully encrypted services more recently. Digital innovation helped such firms build rapidly expanding user communities. Not everything needs to be in the digital space; examples exist in conventional spheres too. A motor pump can be continuously improved for multi-stage performance and graded power consumption; a water submersible pump, however, is a breakthrough technological idea. A laptop battery charger can be continuously improved for the charging efficiency, power consumption and form factor; however, a technology which draws back the laptop's heat and recharges the battery would be a niche technology.

Sometimes non-linear ideas have their roots in the basic and oft ignored or forgotten natural configurations. Most of the Internet firms and search engine firms are dependent on vast server farms, established on expansive tracts of land. Tesla's electric car revolution would hinge on a massive battery factory ("giga factory") with adjacent solar and wind farms, making Tesla as much a huge power storage company as a premium electric vehicle company. In future, just as Sun provides free solar power as nature's gift to the mankind, manmade balloons and satellites may be designed and launched to provide wifi connectivity all over the world. Solar power on ground and on rooftops is commonplace; the next horizon lies in floating solar power from seas and oceans. Technologists and business persons may, in future, learn more from nature with inventiveness, and offer new public services with affordability and humility. Conventionally, technologies have tended to influence new user lifestyles. Non-linear technologies, such as artificial intelligence and robotics, would increasingly align with human body as well as nature to develop game changing (and life changing) products and services. Newer technologies would follow human thoughts and physical capabilities to invent new niche products that could improve human life and environmental management in an almost limitless manner.

Technological Efficiency, Financial Sufficiency

Embracing a niche idea to serve life or nature, converting the idea into a product using new or existing technology and influencing customers to use them, together, is often in the capability of technology-driven start-up firms. Large firms have the ability to innovate new products in a linear fashion, for example from simple Positron Emission Tomography (PET) to PET combined with Computed Tomography (CT) or with Magnetic Resonance Imaging (MRI). In each combination, the number of slices could increase across generations of equipment (say, from 64 to 360) or the efficiency of 3 D imaging could be enhanced. These developments are best done by the medical equipment giants such as GE, Philips and Hitachi. However, the very basis of PET in the original past had been university level researches in the late 1950s (University of Pennsylvania, Washington University School of Medicine, Massachusetts

General Hospital and Brookhaven National Laboratory, for example).

Futuristic radical biomedical technologies in this domain could be non-linear. Nuclear medicine and imaging studies require a radio-isotope tracer (or, a radio pharmaceutical) being injected into the blood stream for imaging. If there were to be new technologies that make a constituent of the blood itself or the blood volume and flow rate themselves descriptors of the imaging study, there could emerge a totally new generation of non-interventionist, bio-friendly non-nuclear medical diagnostic equipment. Novel genetic and immuno-markers could predict risks of cardiac, neurological and cellular diseases. Newer, non-linear technologies in any domain make for life-changing efficiency. However, technological efficiency requires financial sufficiency to germinate and grow. As seen by the PET example, public funding of such universities and research grants made such technological innovation possible. However, firms which licensed the technologies had the financial capability to mass-produce the products and also achieve increasing levels of technological efficiency in such equipment. In a technologically virtuous world, the universe of collective technology ideas would be far greater than the canvas of individual funding opportunities. The academic, industrial and business ecosystems must evolve in a manner of combining technological efficiency and financial sufficiency.

From Start-up to Ramp-up, from Passion to Fusion

The above discussion brings us back to the examples that were reviewed at the beginning of this chapter. Successful start-ups have technological efficiency but they need financial solvency to validate their entrepreneurial theorems and ramp up their business models. While the examples discussed herein are dramatic indicators of the practice and potential in the technology space, routinely hundreds of decrepit as well as robust start-ups get acquired or co-share and license their technologies to enable the growth of start-ups. It is a virtuous, even if occasionally chaotic and brazenly capitalistic, world as technological efficiency and financial sufficiency seek the synergy of each other. The point at which the synergistic marriage gets made in each case is a matter of considered judgment and reasoned risk-taking. Despite the virtuosity of this equation, many times an inability to objectively introspect on the part of the brilliant start-ups and an inability to perceptively prospect on the part of the financial behemoths act to derail the virtuous process.

Not to be outdone, big firms do try to set up mini-laboratories, incubators and venture teams to clone the start-up innovation culture organically within their large monolithic structures. However, behemoths tend to be more adept at scaling up product lines and businesses rapidly rather than patiently nurturing potential ideas and products. External start-ups would continue to be the most important resource for innovation and new business. The inventiveness and passion of technologists and entrepreneurs would continue to be responsible for converting new ideas into innovative products and then onto scalable businesses. When inventiveness matures into practicality and passion accepts stability on the part of start-ups, and when institutional ego respects external technologies and clinical analytics subserves futuristic visions on the part of corporate majors, they become the vital time-points of intersection for the start-ups and the acquiring firms, respectively. The synergistic equation of adding technological efficiency and financial solvency for sustainable growth delivers maximum value when the timing is right, and mutual competencies are well-understood, well-respected and well-supported in the pre- and post-acquisition scenarios.

CHAPTER 9

Entrepreneurial Academics

Science, Technology, Entrepreneurship, Management, and Studentship (STEMS): A Transformational Paradigm for India

A nation's competitive advantage is built by its scientific and technological innovation on one hand and its managerial and entrepreneurial ethic on the other. As India aspires to become the third largest economy in the globe by 2035, the above four factors, enhanced by the new graduate stock, would need to be the key drivers of the transformation. In the past, India has been losing its bright scientists and engineers to greener pastures abroad. With India poised to become the third largest economy in the world, this trend should logically be reversed, with more overseas citizens trying to contribute to the Indian economic transformation. More particularly, it will be the commitment of bright scientists and engineers of India to stay in India, or return to India after their post-graduation and research studies abroad, that would make India an industrial and economic superpower.

India is no longer content with just being the world's back-office. The country is fast moving into the arena of global manufacturing and design, including spacecraft and defence equipment. In fact, smart science and frugal engineering are the new buzz words that are gaining acceptance as concepts that are typically Indian. The ability of the Indian scientists to invent new processes and discover new drug candidates at fractional time and cost has already drawn the interest of global pharmaceutical industry. The ability of the country's engineers to design and establish projects in the shortest possible time with low investment costs and their creativity to design functional products with different value points is getting recognized globally. Scientists and engineers, therefore, have a great opportunity with the kind of transformation and expectation anchored around 'Make in India.'

Science and Technology

Science and technology (or engineering) are the twin pillars on which a nation's economic progress and social development are built. All the developed nations owe their progress to the fundamental contributions of their scientists and engineers whose inventions and discoveries led to creation of new product and business lines. Science is a systematic study of the behaviour of the physical world with discovery, theorization and experimentation constantly expanding the envelope of knowledge. Engineering is the domain of applying science to design, develop, build and maintain equipment, facilities and infrastructure as well as operate production systems to deliver products and services. Both science and engineering are inspired by a spirit of enquiry, a philosophy of detail and an ethic of commitment. These great disciplines teach a student to be data based and yet innovative and creative. Emphasis on quality and safety are an integral part of science and technology.

Modern Indian science and technology have traditionally focused on followership. While several institutions specializing in new domains are set up and diverse projects of national importance taken up in India, results have been less than satisfactory due to non-fostering of a culture of innovation. The problem is accentuated by lack of funding and low compensation and incentive structures in the research field. Even institutes of national importance such as the Indian Institutes of Technology and Indian Institute of Science as well as laboratories of Council of Scientific and Industrial Research have not been able to come up with commercially viable patented new technologies. For example, according to statistics released by the World Intellectual Property Organization (WIPO) for global patent filings in 2015, India filed only 1423 patent applications compared to China's 29846, Japan's 44235 and US's 57385. In addition, most of the patents of China, Japan and US are in high technology sectors. The good news, however, is that infrastructure and talent pool for a greater intellectual thrust exists in India. The challenge is one of sparking the research interest with strategic direction, performance management and incentive development.

Entrepreneurship and Management

Science and technology constitute the core of a nation but entrepreneurship and management are the catalysts for application of science and technology for human endeavour. A great nation can be built only by entrepreneurship, which creates new lines of activity, new areas of business, new enterprises and even new industries based on entrepreneurial ideas and passion. Entrepreneurship is typically based on new, innovative products and services, improved and more efficient manufacturing processes, and/or novel and creative delivery of products and services to customers. Whatever be the domain of value chain which houses entrepreneurship, innovative use of science and technology lies at the core of entrepreneurship. The wide canvas where entrepreneurship can make its mark has no limits at all. Established and new product lines as well as sunset and sunrise product lines all qualify for entrepreneurial development. More often than not, the start-up entrepreneurial effort is individual or small group driven focusing on innovation in various fields.

Management has long been realized as the interdisciplinary and interfaculty approach that applies and utilizes all forms of capital, human, machine and financial, to generate value for the firms, investors, society and the nation through products and services. The growth and value creation of successful organizations, even of entrepreneurial organizations after their initial success, is clearly attributable to good management. The decline and value erosion of failed organizations is similarly attributable to bad management. While good management is a part of successful entrepreneurship, management, in one sense, takes over where entrepreneurship leaves; from initial local success to sustainable global scale-up and from the first specialization to eventual integration or diversification. One of the important tasks and great challenges of management is finding the right blend of technical and human factors. Successful management is also one of evolving its own model, contextually relevant to the company, society and nation.

India's Opportunities and Challenges

India has tremendous strengths with its vast pool of scientists and technologists as well as its fast developing managerial and entrepreneurial base. As a result, India ought to have been a major industrial and economic power by now. However, economic and industrial policies of post-independence India, close to a very long period of 45 years between 1947 and 1992, followed a highly socialistic and regulated pattern. Most decisions to create capacity, whether in education or industry, were limited by resource availability rather than revenue generation and by demand control rather than market expansion. While a great measure of self-reliance, economic independence and scientific and technological maturity was achieved as a result, India lagged behind in economic and innovation indices. The initial stirrings of industrial rediscovery became evident from the 1980s when Indian industrialists began to turn externally oriented, and from the 1990s when the government embarked upon economic liberalization. The economic growth rate has in the past few years doubled to an average of 9 percent per annum, from the previous historical long term, multi-decade average of 4.5 percent.

While there has been a quantitative expansion of capacities in India post-liberalization, with a flood of new products and services, from automobiles to aircraft and from flat panel televisions to cellular phones, most of it is consumption driven. The internal processors and operating systems of most products as well as some high technology products are still based on imports from more advanced nations. The Indian automobile industry may have absorbed the imported product technologies and manufacturing processes but most of the sophisticated equipment from machining centres to robotic welders are still imported. The Indian pharmaceutical industry could be the largest exporter of medicines to the most advanced countries but the laboratory and manufacturing equipment are of imported pedigree in such lines. India excels in software but has not yet produced a search engine, social network, drone or artificial intelligence bot. Science, technology, entrepreneurship and management have to share equal responsibility for the current state of sub-optimization of India's potential. The new NDA Government's policy of Make in India has both its opportunity and challenge neatly cut out.

Back to Basics, a Leap into Future

India's IT and manufacturing outsourcing consumption would sustain a consumption driven market expansion and entry of several new products which are hereafter indigenously manufactured, assembled through completely knocked down (CKD) and semi knocked (SKD) route or even as imported completely built units (CBU). However, India as the world's third largest economy cannot afford to rest with a linear scale-up of current capabilities and approaches. There is a need for transformational shift. This shift must have two approaches. The first relates to a focus on fundamentals in science and technology and the second relates to a qualitative boost to the Indian managerial and entrepreneurial capabilities. In both, entrepreneurship and start-up culture have a critical part.

Scientists and technologists of India need to direct a portion of their intellectual efforts to drive fundamental innovations. One model could be to differentiate between organizations dedicated to fundamental innovation and those focused on followership or application of innovation. This is best accomplished in certain industries such as automobiles, pharmaceuticals and in research space. Most other industries, however, require co-development of fundamental innovation and applied innovation. For example, it would be impractical for an architectural firm to design only green and novel buildings or for an automobile firm to manufacture only electric cars. Commencing fundamental innovations in niche areas and mass customizing them later is a challenge for scientists, technologists, managers and entrepreneurs.

Any level of science and technology planning cannot be actualized without matching resources. There could be three ways to support this endeavour, one through wholly public investments, second through wholly private investments and the third through public-private partnerships. The aggregate investment on fundamental research should be at least 10 percent of gross domestic product, whether coming through public, private or joint methodologies. As one is aware, innovation-led companies devote 15 to 20 percent of their turnover to research and development as a whole. Governments and industry associations need to chalk out a strategic plan for fundamental research as guidance for the industry and governments.

Similarly, there must be a focus on the fundamentals of robust management and creative entrepreneurship. Indian management has of late been gaining international recognition for its end-to-end conceptualization, risk-integrated decision making, creative multitasking, and speedy execution. The model, however, needs to be more deepened and broad-based to cover every enterprise and agency. Management institutions would need to take the lead by dedicating at least one semester of the typical two year management courses to management studies that are contextually relevant for India. It is time that Indian management is translated from an abstract approach realized by only a few to a tangible construct accessible to all.

And most certainly, entrepreneurship needs a major boost to support the transformation of the Indian industry and economy. Entrepreneurship could occur at any level and at any age. While young graduates are often encouraged to become entrepreneurs rather than job seekers the whole employment and retirement system should have flexibility and fluidity to encourage entrepreneurship at any point of time in one's career, including post-retirement. For example, working managers and leaders could be encouraged to take up parts of industrial value chain as entrepreneurial ventures. Corporate entities need to establish entrepreneurship endowment funds and corpuses to support such entrepreneurial forays. Yet another mode could be to offer additional retirement funds to high performance executives linked solely to their commitment to set up entrepreneurial firms.

From 'STEM' to 'STEMS'

Clearly, Science, Technology, Entrepreneurship and Management (STEM) model is the basic foundation of a nation's economic and industrial progress. India, however, has as its forte a fifth dimension as it seeks to be transformative over the next 20 years. This relates to India's very young demographic profile (30 percent of population aged below 15 years) and the vast educational infrastructure that could be quantitatively and qualitatively expanded. While the early Indian governments laid the foundations of a highly regulated and capacity constrained higher educational system, entry of private sector into the engineering and science college system in the 1980s has provided a major impetus to the education scenario in terms of quantitative easing.

India has presently a uniquely large educational base out of Tier 1 and Tier 2 cities, which needs to be upgraded and diversified into rural satellite centres. In spite of a relatively low overall literacy score at primary level (which itself needs further improvement from the current 74 percent), India has one of the largest talent pools in the world, which needs to be leveraged more fully. India has, for example, around 2.5 million graduates passing out every year, of which more than 700,000 are science and mathematics graduates, 750,000 are post-graduates, and 800,000 are engineers. India with its vast network of over 400 universities, 14000 colleges and 1500 research institutions has contributed to the development of the second largest pool of scientists and engineers (of over 60 million) in the world.

As students are taught to become scientists, engineers and managers, the right experiential learning structures and inputs on creativity, innovation, management and entrepreneurship would build capabilities and enhance confidence in them to take up entrepreneurship. If even 10% of the scientists and engineers graduating each year in India choose to become entrepreneurs with unique ideas in the chosen field, the student force would be really transforming India. This is not to say that entrepreneurship is the only route to fulfilment of a larger purpose in life. The key here is being entrepreneurial. Whatever the avocation chosen by a student, whether as a laboratory scientist, shop floor engineer, product developer, information technologist or even a business analyst, the focus should be on being entrepreneurial in thinking and execution.

For student entrepreneurship to succeed, research and manufacturing establishments as well as businesses must be more open to accepting and trusting students as interns and providing them with challenging projects of long duration rather than paper studies of short duration. The highly successful model of medical internship must be made mandatory in engineering education as well, with industries required to take on board students as understudies to scientists, technologists and managers. This will strengthen the ability of students to understand and cope up with real world industrial complexities. When this happens, STEMS, the science, technology, entrepreneurship, management and studentship framework, would be a well-balanced five component transformative model for India.

STEMS as a Collaborative Paradigm

Today's globalized world is highly competitive. India, despite the global attention and adulation it is receiving, has some way to go to attain the super economic power status. The good news is that a fast growing market and a highly youthful society are geared to make the transformation happen. India needs to innovate for its own new products and services, besides constantly enhancing the value of all current products and services. India should lead the world in upholding quality, protecting safety, reducing costs and eliminating waste. At the same time, once in few years Indian industry and business may have to reinvent themselves with completely new ways of doing things to achieve new levels in global competitiveness. As India opens its doors to 100 percent direct foreign investment in hitherto insulated areas such as aviation and defence, global majors would establish their bases in India, hoping to leverage India's talent base in an entrepreneurial way.

Such a transformative journey cannot happen by only the individual efforts of scientists, technologists, managers or entrepreneurs. India needs to move towards an ideal national system of mutually collaborative science, technology, entrepreneurship and management, each of them progressing with vertical and horizontal linkages, all the way from student days. For example, in a collaborative framework innovations in material sciences would lead to better engineering of components while better designs of equipment and tooling would lead to better components from designs. Simultaneously, managers would need to plan component changes as part of model makeovers strategically and entrepreneurs would need to lead such transformative inflexions in science, technology and management on a continuous basis. From the current diffused and random resort to science, technology, entrepreneurship and management, a more holistic and integrated emphasis on the five component model of building a great new educational system on 'science, technology, entrepreneurship, management and studentship' (STEMS) is well merited for India in its transformative journey as an economic superpower.

CHAPTER 10

Family-Entrepreneur-Professional Triad

Managing Family-Entrepreneur Companies: Challenges of a Professional CEO

With the increasing emphasis on corporate governance and an enlightened interest in business development, many family and entrepreneur led firms as well as start-up firms are hiring professional Chief Executive Officers (CEOs) to run their businesses. This is opening up new exciting career opportunities for capable professional managers. However, this has as many pitfalls as opportunities. This chapter summarizes four critical facets of this transition.

Coping with the Family/Entrepreneur

Typically, a family tends to be conservative while an entrepreneur tends to overreach. A family member or an entrepreneur, continuing as an executive head of the board, could therefore be a major constraint on a professional CEO's style. The answer to this from a CEO does not lie in attempting to change the family member's or entrepreneur's business DNA. It lies in the CEO's ability to offer a framework by which unreasonable aspirations and reasonable resources are harmonized to develop a workable blue-print for the future.

An organization in transition (from family-promoter control to professional management) needs intensive and structured interfaces at all levels, more so at the top, to smoothen the transition. An entrepreneur CEO and a professional CEO would most likely have dissimilar aspirations, managerial styles and personalities. The professional CEO would need to constantly evaluate how his relationship develops with the family / entrepreneur on one hand and the organization on the other hand. Only frequent and direct communication with the family and entrepreneur can help usher in the transition smoothly.

In an organization controlled or co-promoted by more than one family member or entrepreneur, the *inter-se* dynamics between the family members or co-promoters are not always visible. The apparently passive member(s) may have invisible influencing power, which needs to be understood. Similarly, an existing organization may have persons of influence who do not operate in the open. Moulding all these relations in his or her favour is a challenge for the professional CEO. The entrepreneur and the family have a major responsibility in ensuring that such elements do not diffuse the focus and thwart the effectiveness of the CEO.

A family or entrepreneur run organization is likely to have many informal channels of communication between various employees and the family member or entrepreneur, which operate as a result of the micro-management of the company by the family or the entrepreneur. The informal channels could often distort information and even use the information for ends which are not necessarily aligned to business goals. The CEO would need to establish structured strategic planning and budgeting processes, visible performance management systems and open communication channels as a formal means that renders the informal operations increasingly irrelevant. All of these must, of course, be contextually appropriate to the entrepreneurial nature of the company.

Keeping up the Growth Momentum

As one moves into a CEO's position of a hitherto family run or entrepreneur driven company, the challenges would be significant in the areas of project execution, operations management, strategic planning, business development, peer-relationships and communication with investors and employees. The focus and spirit of the role would need to be on managing for the future with the speed of an entrepreneur and the caution of a family. The CEO would need to innovate constantly on business, technical and operational models to achieve this. The knowledge, assets and execution capabilities of the past and present, though belonging to different businesses and products, often serve as the levers for new business development. These must be exploited on a proactive basis. At the same time, old business models and past experiences of established companies need not necessarily succeed in a family / entrepreneur company. The CEO has to be, therefore, dynamic, contextual and differentiated in respect of strategy as well as execution.

While the very reason for bringing in a CEO into a family firm is to do things differently, yet when it comes to systemic changes, the entrepreneur or the family would more likely evade rather than support the changes, ostensibly for fear of losing business momentum or stability as the case may be. Yet, as a CEO, one has to live with apparent contradictions; closing down manufacturing lines while investing in new facilities, slashing jobs while creating new knowledge positions, phasing out products while innovating new ones, eliminating today's expenses while adding costs for the future and so on. Building long term value, without compromise to current revenue and profit growth is the essence of the CEO task.

Fusion of strategic intuition with operational excellence, and balancing of the short term with the long term are the ultimate challenges for a CEO. A family or entrepreneur-led company would have achieved growth due to an opportunistic mix of operational and business strategies. This may not meet a professional CEO's litmus test in all cases. Practically viewed, neither time nor resources will be on the CEO's side to attempt a total structural, systemic and value-chain upgrade of a hitherto family or promoter run firm. The CEO is likely to succeed if he keeps the degree of revamp to a minimum even as he judiciously pursues newer options that comply with professional norms, both in technical and business arenas.

The responsibilities of a CEO would typically follow a normal distribution. About seventy percent of the focus would need to be on the core aspects of driving revenue and profitability. There would be two outlying areas of say, fifteen percent each, related to turnaround (extreme cost and efficiency management) and family or promoter inspired value-gaming (extreme futuristic investment bets). A focus on the outlying areas beyond the limits indicated could expose a CEO to the threat of weakened performance on the core.

In today's competitive world, investors (including the promoters) have a relentless focus on continued growth in revenues and profits. Unless there is a need for a radical restructuring, ways and means have to be found by the CEO to keep growing, even while rectifying errant operations. If any part of the business requires radical restructuring with organizational implications or large investments with long lead times, the plan must be clearly articulated to the stakeholders so that there are no misunderstandings.

The domain of business development is almost always imprecise. As strategic business development is a key responsibility of a CEO, he would need an organizational infrastructure for a structured yet entrepreneurial business development. In business development, by definition and practice, the entrepreneur tends to over-commit. The family member, on the other hand, tends to be conservative and cash-conscious. The professional CEO, however, has to balance these trends by arranging resources and ensuring execution.

Reshaping the Organization

The effectiveness of a CEO lies in the smartness of delegation, notwithstanding the possibility that the informal or unstructured nature of the organization requires his close attention. The CEO cannot afford to have all "pupils" and no "masters," if he wishes to succeed fast. A CEO has also to make sure that the persons to whom responsibilities are being delegated are good enough for the job. For delegation to be effective, the overall level of competence (both individually and collectively) has to meet stringent standards. Effective delegation also requires that various departments at all levels interact meaningfully without 'upward delegation' which is characteristic of organizations functioning as vertical silos requiring sanctions from the top for everything. Cross-functional teams will need to be encouraged at all levels to enable executives broaden their horizons, without the day-to-day involvement of the CEO or even the next tier. While speed of execution is important, issues have to be prioritized. A smart CEO would use multiple levers differently, to blend delegation with accountability.

When a new chief takes over a family or entrepreneur run firm, people who have been wayward or powerful hitherto in the organization tend to be defensive or manipulative. There can be no implicit belief in anyone until his professional competencies and managerial approaches are established. Setting uniformly clear goals would be one way to isolate performers from non-performers. The concept of a long grace period could be as detrimental as bundling all the old guard as being irrelevant. An objective judgement on each executive and checking out with the entrepreneur or family would be a quick and effective route to aligning the organization to the CEO's thoughts.

While the board deliberations in general tend to be more a matter of form than substance, the boards of some family or promoter companies may have an even greater issue with regard to the independence. With corporate governance coming into vogue, from a regulatory as well as a process perspective, one has to hope that such boards will ensure objective and strategic oversight on corporate matters. The professional CEO will need to add his inputs specifically to enliven and spark the discussions, even though he may be constrained by what the family member or entrepreneur has been disclosing so far to the board.

Though in an organization the buck certainly stops at the CEO, all onus cannot be on the CEO alone. For the organization to really reap the value from a professional CEO, the family member or the entrepreneur would also need to fulfil certain responsibilities. For example, he has to respect the mandate given to the CEO, explain the past and integrate his experience with the new CEO's perspective, follow the CEO's advice in matters of strategic plan and operational execution, eliminate invisible or whimsical checks on the CEO's style and create forums for free flow of information.

Dealing with Oneself

A CEO who is new to the job would need to ensure that his time gets channelled to activities which are most productive for the physical and financial performance of his company. Even though teaching and coaching are an integral part of a good CEO's profile, the CEO cannot allow them to erode his ability to focus on other key factors relevant to his new position. Consolidation of his own position should be as important as coaching others at least until he gets a solid grip on the company affairs.

The hallmark of a true CEO is that he outgrows his functional core competence. In several respects, he demonstrates that he is "equi-distant" with all functions and all professionals. Similarly he "owns" all the functions, whether or not they work for him, against him or with him. This is easier said than done. It requires a constant work-out on oneself to achieve this state of mind. A CEO, in the event he is from a technical background, will definitely need to become financially savvy as well. Similarly, a non-technical CEO has to demonstrate certain grasp of the technical nuances of the business to gain an overall organizational command. In addition, any CEO would benefit from tracking the successes and failures of other CEOs. Such readings would help him raise the bar of performance on one hand and develop a sense of equanimity about the limits of performance on the other.

Ultimately, all stakeholders, the family or the entrepreneur and the board need assurance that things are moving fine. Regardless of the past track record of the CEO and his current level of confidence in the new job, the CEO needs to periodically assure his stakeholders regarding corporate performance and investor returns. The longer the gestation period of a project or the more traumatic the nature of a change, the greater would be the need for such assurance. Often, written reports value-added by face-to-face discussions tend to reinforce such confidence all-round. The CEO will also need to significantly work on his presentation skills as well as his diplomatic approaches which are as important as the raw results of operations. The CEO, though an apex leader, is as dependent as others in the organization in some respects, for example - resources. He cannot be a silent sufferer for the corporate mission when resources are not available. He has as much responsibility for demanding (or generating/deploying) capital as he has for delivering on achievements. It is not *infra dig* for a CEO to demand the due resource inputs for the business from the board, the family or the promoters.

The CEO's role in creating a positive organizational culture, conceptualizing a growth-oriented business model, developing a new corporate plan and driving a tight execution program would be vital in determining his impact on the hitherto family or entrepreneur run organization. If a CEO desires to make a lasting impact beyond the level of his past achievements, he would also need to do something that rivets attention. Given India's niche in the knowledge-led activities and the several business opportunities waiting to be tapped in these areas, fundamental innovation would be a key driver. It certainly calls for resources, skills and equally importantly, time. However, unless the seed is sown one day and carefully nourished every day thereafter, the professional CEO and his company (in transition from the hitherto family or promoter led status) will not have the comfort of lasting shade in the future.

CHAPTER 11

Entrepreneurial Culture

National Entrepreneurial Culture: Systemic and Mind-set Factors

Widespread industrial and economic development of a nation is triggered by entrepreneurial initiatives in the country. India, which is recognized today globally for its educated and hardworking human resource base, needs to focus its sights on harnessing entrepreneurial spirit for enhanced economic and social development. This chapter discusses several approaches to ignite the entrepreneurial spirit with widespread positive impact for India.

Entrepreneurship Anchors

An entrepreneur is someone who starts his or her own business, especially when such activity involves risks. The risks relate primarily to market acceptance of business proposition, arrangement of requisite capital, creation of organization and uncertainty of financial returns. An entrepreneur mitigates the risks by developing a unique proposition for his venture in terms of product or service innovation and/or cost arbitrage relative to a larger organization. An ability to address and manage risks is a key entrepreneurial anchor. The risk taking ability is of an even greater importance when the entrepreneur is a first generation entrepreneur and when the start-up founder has no family engine to power him.

The combination of innovativeness and competitiveness that is implicit in an entrepreneurial activity acts as the key trigger for broader industrial and economic development. A study of industrial history points out that each and every global corporation has had its roots in entrepreneurial activity; from Henry Ford's Ford Motor to Akio Morita's Sony. That said, it has also been a natural phenomenon for established business houses to start their own entrepreneurial initiatives through diversification projects. While such initiatives lack the main ingredient of a typical entrepreneurial activity viz., personal risk-taking of a promoter, such growth initiatives do involve risks on other multiple dimensions, and contribute in an equal measure to accelerated industrial and economic development.

Entrepreneurship in Curriculum

The Indian education and social system is typically geared towards secured jobs, particularly in large organizations. Educational streams are pursued based on potential employment opportunities, regardless of the aptitude and flair of the students. Very few, if at all, of the students are tuned towards starting their own business or non-business enterprises. It is important therefore that Indian curriculum from the early schooling days incorporates entrepreneurship as a core subject of curriculum. History has instances of brilliant inventors, whether Alexander Fleming who discovered Penicillin or Graham Bell who discovered telephone, laying foundations of great business empires. The Indian educational system needs creative economic historians who can interpret the history of industrial innovations and business creativity across generations, and identify core entrepreneurial initiatives, as case studies of inspiration, that transformed business and economy over time.

As a student progresses from a school to a college and later to a professional institution and a university, it becomes appropriate to inculcate the entrepreneurial approach through specific projects. The project work that needs to be undertaken by a student in a real life or business setting, in partial fulfilment of the graduate or post-graduate study requirements, provides an important avenue for entrepreneurial development. Unfortunately, this system has been reduced, over time, to a grudgingly tolerated formality by both the academic institutions and business undertakings. There is a clear need to revitalize and redefine the system of project work to fulfil a larger entrepreneurial purpose that a project work can truly deliver.

A reputed business school in India has recently initiated a process by which some of its students could work with industry icons as their understudies. This practice, the school felt, could enable them gain valuable insights into leadership styles. What is perhaps even more urgently required is a system by which graduate and post-graduate students are encouraged to work on establishing pilot scale industrial or business projects based on co-guidance from the academic institutions and business enterprises.

Teams of people from technical and managerial disciplines from within an institution as well as from different technical and business management institutions (say, from IITs and IIMs, to start with) can combine to undertake such projects. This methodology would, of course, require a sea change in how the institutions approach project work as part of their academic curriculum and how they would provide credits to individual and group work. A revitalized academic industrial initiative of entrepreneurial projects would prepare the students exceedingly well on the entrepreneurial journey.

Entrepreneurship at Work

An executive, manager or leader in an established undertaking could be entrepreneurial at work as well, notwithstanding the fact that one is bound by structure, systems and processes in taking decisions and executing them. Being an entrepreneur does not mean being all alone, taking all decisions individually or taking risks all upon oneself. Even an entrepreneur would need to create a vision, strategy, structure and process with a team and raise finances through articulation of the concept to the potential stakeholders. The challenge for an executive at work to undertake new developments, construct new projects, introduce new products or foray into new markets is no different. The challenge even for a corporate executive is one of identifying a new domain based on one's own experience, expertise, risk-taking ability and communication skills. Entrepreneurial executives can help companies expand and diversify their businesses, reaching higher career heights in the process.

Entrepreneurship at work does, however, require an appropriate organizational eco-system. Entrepreneurially vibrant organizations, in fact, are distinctly differentiated from bureaucratically pedestrian organizations. Leaders and managers in entrepreneurial organizations tend to encourage scientists, technologists and other professionals take risks in setting up new projects or venturing into new domains. There exists palpable latitude in such organizations towards forgiving genuine mistakes or accepting unanticipated outcomes. This objectivity nurtures the ability of people to undertake risky but potentially rewarding projects. Such organizations balance the rigidity of structure and process with the flexibility of innovation and creativity. This requires an organizational culture in which the entire leadership team is committed and aligned towards being entrepreneurial at work. Organizations could create entrepreneurship councils as a formal means to encourage executives, managers and leaders take entrepreneurial decisions, as distinct from those related to regular operations and normal business continuity projects.

Entrepreneurship at the Helm

One would imagine that having an entrepreneur at the helm is one of the best ways to promote the continued entrepreneurial growth of the corporation that he helped to conceptualize and grow. One may even conclude that an organization which has an entrepreneur-founder at the helm as the Chief Executive Officer (CEO) would be the most entrepreneurial, always exploring new avenues. Unfortunately, however, several entrepreneurial organizations as they grow larger tend to become deliberative, if not bureaucratic. They tend to take strategic decisions (for example, integration, diversification, divestiture and acquisition) in a structured manner within the defined industry boundary. The entrepreneur who is also the CEO in such organizations gets bound by accountability to his shareholders and investors and finds it difficult to take apparently radical business and investment decisions, especially if they are unrelated to the current business, in an entrepreneurial manner. Getting stuck as an entrepreneur at the helm of a corporation is possibly not the best way to replicate, in broader domains and with greater resources, what the same entrepreneur could achieve in a much narrower domain and with a much smaller resource base.

The logical solution for the entrepreneurial plateau in decision making seems to lie in each entrepreneur making a decision on continuing to be an entrepreneurial leader vis-à-vis becoming a professional leader. Whether to head and manage his corporation or remain a mere investor turning over the reins of his corporation to a full-fledged professional is a healthy dilemma which every entrepreneur must face from time to time. Remaining as an entrepreneur, choosing to move away from day to day management, would help the entrepreneur to refocus his energies and resources on newer entrepreneurial ventures. The business models, investor regulations and economic system that dominate the Indian business system are unfortunately not conducive to entrepreneurs establishing newer ventures. In addition, the Indian entrepreneur tends to get emotionally and physically attached to the company he created, often failing to see the larger role he could play in national wealth building. The American culture, on the other hand, is one of entrepreneurs creating value, monetizing it and moving on with new business lives. The American entrepreneurial culture has clearly led to a continuous creation of newer and more challenging businesses of greater value in the US economy. This is perhaps a more appropriate model if India has to utilize effectively its scarce entrepreneurial talent. A true entrepreneur would need to be a serial entrepreneur rather than a static entrepreneur in this model.

Entrepreneurship as CSR

To provide a sustainable fillip to the entrepreneurial movement in the country, corporations need to take up development of entrepreneurs as a corporate social responsibility (CSR). Apart from encouraging induction of entrepreneurially trained graduates and post-graduates into companies, and enabling entrepreneurship at work, corporations need to take up moulding of entrepreneurs as a core social responsibility. This could occur in two ways, both of which are mutually supportive to each other. In the first method, each corporation vows to develop at least a few entrepreneurs out of its workforce or from the general public by outsourcing some of the tasks which it has been doing by itself. For example, a company which has been doing all its equipment maintenance itself may choose to let its maintenance chief form an entrepreneurial venture that maintains facilities and outsource the activity to him. There are similarly several possibilities for large companies to outsource their broader supply chain management activities (including materials planning, procurement and logistics activities) or corporate services activities (including recruitment, accounting, audit, customer relationship management) to entrepreneurial ventures led by their own executives. While such activities may run the risk of breeding collusive cronyism, true entrepreneurial spirit should see such ventures break free of their sponsors and grow on their own sooner than later.

The second way of corporate entrepreneurial responsibility is to reach out to the wider society and enable members of the society to set up their own enterprises. The very process of corporations adopting their neighbourhoods can help the citizens set up a slew of social and economic ventures based on their capabilities. From simple social activities like tailoring and retailing to more involved infrastructure activities like education and business, corporations can, through their corporate social responsibility arms, contribute to an indigent society evolving itself into an entrepreneurial society. As industrial firms seek to expand aggressively through new industrial campuses and economic zones, the need to support the society with more sustainable means than one-time cash remuneration for the acquired land is self-evident. Typically, companies undertake corporate social responsibility activities only after securing of their business and operations as is evident by the late stage contributions made in this sphere by established companies. However, by integrating corporate entrepreneurial responsibility as part of their entry strategy in new green field projects the companies can seek synergy between industrial development and social equity.

Summary

With over ten million graduates, post-graduates and research scholars graduating annually from colleges, institutions and universities of higher education in India, the potential to develop and unleash the entrepreneurial energy of the vast educated work force is immense. Even if a small percentage of the educated human resource base opts to establish its own entrepreneurial ventures, the employment and development triggers for the Indian economy would be immense. This, however, requires significant systemic and mind-set changes. From ingraining self-reliance and entrepreneurship as an early family and educational ethic to the development of an industrial and economic system that encourages entrepreneurship both at work and outside work, a host of systemic and cultural changes are required in the vast spectrum to achieve the full potential of a highly literate and highly entrepreneurial educated India.

CHAPTER 12

Financial Entrepreneurship

Nano to Mega Entrepreneurial Spectrum: Need for Financial Entrepreneurs

Enterprises emerge from entrepreneurial energy. Entrepreneurs fight against odds to create entities that can convert ideas into products or services. An entrepreneurial journey involves several challenges including, but not limited to, the conceptualization of the entrepreneurial initiative, arrangement of finances, assembling of the team, establishment of the project, delivery of the product or service, and finally earning of reasonable returns to please the shareholders (including the entrepreneur). These core, critical steps in the journey of an entrepreneurial enterprise also need to be consistent with the capabilities and potential of the entrepreneur. There is little clarity on when and how the challenge for entrepreneurial journey ends, and the quest for enterprise sustainability begins.

The popular appreciation of entrepreneurial effort tends to be limited to first generation enterprises which have achieved scale and scope, with high visibility in media. Despite such enterprises achieving a significant success relative to the starting milestones, the pressures are ever higher on them to grow beyond boundaries, in a virtually limitless process. In this endeavour, the true creative spirit of an entrepreneurial venture gets overwhelmed by the clinical intellect and aggressive force of such companies in pursuit of growth. Pursuit of scale and scope, no doubt, transforms the entrepreneurs heading such firms into global business leaders but also limits them from institutionalizing their intellectual talent on a wider entrepreneurial base, as a national comparative advantage.

Infosys Insight; Foresight for Growth

A brief study of Infosys Technologies Limited, India's leading information technology corporation, and their founders offers certain unique insights and possibilities in this complex interplay of enterprise and entrepreneurship. Infosys was founded in 1981 with a very modest capital of USD 250 by a team of seven software engineers, led by the founder N R Narayana Murthy. The company was in many ways a pioneer in leveraging Indian software talent for providing global information technology solutions. With a singular focus and a creative global delivery model, Infosys never had to look back in its growth journey. Today, Infosys is a corporation listed on NASDAQ with a global IT and Consulting Services business, and with nearly 200,000 employees, revenues of US $9.5 billion and market capitalization of approximately US $43 billion.

Of the seven founders, N S Raghavan retired from the services of Infosys in 1999 as its joint managing director and went on to become a mentor for several entrepreneurs. N R Narayana Murthy continued to nurture Infosys into a global corporation as its chairman, and later as its chief mentor. Logically, a large global corporation such as Infosys with excellent revenue and profitability would have the ability to encourage entrepreneurial entities all across its value chain, and possibly should have created platforms for various entrepreneurs to emerge from within the company. It appears that the founders rather than the company are in the forefront of encouraging entrepreneurship. N R Narayana Murthy had set up a Rs 6 billion (USD133 million) venture capital fund called Catamaran Investment Pvt Limited to encourage entrepreneurial ventures, across sectors.

The establishment of the Murthy-Catamaran venture implies that even a global company may not do more than encourage ancillary entity development in its own value chain, while an entrepreneur who grew such a company can possibly contribute to more broad-based entrepreneurial development as an entrepreneur rather than as a corporate honcho. Indications are that Catamaran would be sector and scale agnostic while investing, which is an encouraging sign. Going beyond Infosys and N R Narayana Murthy (and other Infosys founders who are also into supporting start-ups), however, one needs to recognize that entrepreneurial development could occur in different configurations and formats. Entrepreneurs who tasted success have now the opportunity and option to provide a discrete institutional structure, distinct from the firms that they founded and grew, to provide a genuine and powerful thrust to entrepreneurial development in the country.

Scaling and Scoping; Pathway to Growth

Any enterprise emerges and grows on only two fundamental dimensions: product (service included) and market (geography or customer segment included). Depending on the product range and market spread enterprises get positioned in terms of scale and scope. The modernization of the corporation on a number of collateral and enabling factors such as technology and organization has to serve these two fundamentals. While the entrepreneurial spirit of discovery of product and market niche has always been an integral part of social and economic development, the emergence of the modern corporation has sought to substitute that spirit with systematic quest.

It is imperative that entrepreneurial effort is viewed independent of scale and scope (which are drivers of growth) on one hand, and technology and organization (which are differentiators of growth) on the other. India has traditionally given considerable importance to the development of cottage and small scale industries, essentially through investment and tax incentives. Evolution of large scale industry has been seen as a logical pull for further development of such smaller enterprises. Yet, the whole cottage and small scale enterprise movement has got grounded over the years due to the enterprises and the governments failing to appreciate the product-market interplay. There is a need to redefine the enterprise hierarchy to identify where and how different generations and types of entrepreneurial effort fit best.

From Nano to Mega; a Wide Enterprise Spectrum

Entities which cater to one product group and one small homogenous market segment are best termed as nano enterprises. We see nano enterprises all around us but fail to appreciate how the entrepreneurial effort is surviving despite lack of attention to it by the formal economic system. The vegetable cart vendor who serves the neighbourhood homes, the tailor who meets the clothing needs of the location and the corner grocery shop which provides the food and family items, for example, constitute nano enterprises. A nano enterprise is usually operated by only one individual, the founder or the owner.

A printer who prints multiple products for multiple clients with a printing machine and a small team of assistants, a restaurant which provides multiple cuisines for a multi-ethnic population, a boutique which caters to multiple clothing styles constitute the next level of micro enterprises. When these are upgraded to a network, in each case with better technology and logistics support for larger multi-location coverage, they become small scale firms; a desktop networked printer, a chain of restaurants and a designer clothing studio cum boutique, for example, are typical small scale firms.

A publishing cum printing house, a pan-Indian fast foods restaurant and an apparel manufacturing company all of which in modern times require modern technologies, trained work force and capable management represent medium scale enterprises. All listed national companies with highly organized research, manufacturing and marketing capabilities are the typical large companies; for example, a multimedia corporation with core competencies in print or television media, a ready-to-eat foods company and an end-to-end textile and apparel company typify large companies. Blue chip companies and giant corporations in diverse industrial segments with global scale and scope, constitute mega corporations.

The efficiency with which each enterprise operates (for example, the number of households the vegetable vendor can cater to in a day) and the speed with which a firm can morph from one stage to the next higher stages (for example, transit through the growth chain, from being a cart vendor, grocery shop or tailor to becoming a retail chain) is a function of entrepreneurial energy, duly supported by finance and management. The indigent nano entrepreneur, if equipped with a semi-motorized cart, can cover more neighbourhoods. Finance and management can make an aggressive local retailer become a national multi-brand retail chain.

Idea to Enterprise; Passion to Performance

From the yesteryears' business magazine idea to yesterday's direct-to-home television, true entrepreneurial effort is not one of a product or service whose time has come but of an idea which has been thought of ahead of its time. With the explosion in knowledge levels and the implosion in customer needs there exist today far more product and service ideas than at any point of history. Mentorship and financing are two critical inputs which can help the nano, micro and small enterprises get established first, and later become medium, large and mega enterprises progressively. While large firms have the necessary track record and competencies to raise resources for new entrepreneurial ventures in their quest for growth, nano, micro and small firms need explicit, dedicated and empathetic support.

India does not have angel investors. The financing and investment eco-system in India is not specifically geared to spot entrepreneurs and help them translate their ideas into enterprises or organized activities. Established venture capital firms and private equity funds cater to large firms, and only occasionally to medium firms. In India, nano, micro and small firms can emerge and survive only based on conservative bank priority funding. India therefore needs a wholly new genre of entrepreneurial financing, whether it is a uniquely Indian type or an established Western type. There is a need for a new breed of financial entrepreneurs to emerge and lead a whole new entrepreneurial revolution in India. Several alternative models, all of them relevant to different types of entrepreneurial initiatives need to be simultaneously considered as below.

(a) Individual financing model

The ability to finance nano entrepreneurial ventures exists among all earning members of the society, especially the high net-worth individuals (HNIs). The investment required for a vegetable vendor to acquire a modern cart, for a tailor to add a multi-purpose sewing machine and the corner grocery shop to have its own brand of home foods in India would not exceed Rs 20,000 (USD 300) in each case, an amount which is entirely within the means of any earning individual with high savings potential. HNIs, more particularly, should keep a target of creating a few nano-entrepreneurial ventures each year and leave their stamp on the history of entrepreneurial development. Even retired personnel can reinvest a small part of their retirement proceedings to set up their own nano enterprises, be it a corner shop or a core service for the community.

Extending the concept further, gated communities and apartment associations which would have a larger access to collective resources and provide a demand base of captive user needs can help establish nano-entrepreneurial ventures that meet the community needs effectively. From a security service to a mechanized laundry, and from a library service to a documentation service, opportunities for creation of nano ventures by gated residential communities are indeed plenty. As these gated communities develop into new suburbs and mini-cities the nano and micro foundations of business can indeed grow over time. The lesson here is that individuals and communities have far greater power in their hands to create nano entrepreneurs than they realize.

(b) Corporate catalyst model

Major corporations, given their organizational infrastructure and market reach as well as their financial capability can contribute impressively to the entrepreneurial movement directly and indirectly. The logical way is to convert or let go fragments of their value chain or operational spectrum as nano or micro entrepreneurial ventures. This is a natural and economical way of creating entrepreneurial value while enhancing the cost-competitiveness of the company. Each function or domain of a firm, for example research, manufacturing, marketing, supply chain, human resources, accounting, information technology and clinical trials, offers scope for creating entrepreneurial outfits for outsourcing of fragments of such domains.

Yet another way is to leverage a corporation's resources to reach out to wider population, create awareness and harness passion, in association with Non-Governmental Organizations (NGOs) and Not for Profit Organizations (NPOs). The success of the Teach India initiative organized by the Times of India media group in association with select NGOs in bringing together educated experts to teach underprivileged children is proof enough. Corporations can undertake with equal aplomb entrepreneurial initiatives utilizing their resources. In addition to individual corporations industry associations such as FICCI, CII and ASSOCHAM can play a catalyst role by creating divisions for entrepreneurial projects.

(c) Not-for-profit organization model

Not-for-profit organizations (NPOs) headed by passionate leaders can spur and support entrepreneurial initiatives. Bharatiya Yuva Shakti Trust (BYST) is a trend setting model in this context. BYST is a non-profit organization that has been set up in 1992 in India by Lakshmi Venkatesan for providing end-to-end support for disadvantaged micro-entrepreneurs in the form of loans, mentoring, networking and marketing. The young micro-entrepreneurs are nurtured until they reach a level where they are not only self-sufficient, but they in turn make a valuable contribution to the society through creating wealth and employment. Over 4000 experts and professionals associated themselves with BYST as mentors for entrepreneurs. In recent times, actors and public figures have started supporting nano entrepreneurial ventures aimed at poverty alleviation through reality shows in the Indian television channels.

The reach of NPO led initiatives cannot be underestimated. Nationally, BYST has supported 4200 micro-entrepreneurial ventures, employing over 175,000 people and providing training to several thousands of people since its inception. BYST has both rural and urban training programs covering six major regions of India. The Confederation of India (CII) provides the infrastructure and administrative support to BYST. BYST is also networked with international organizations that are aligned to similar objectives. A high point of BYST is its ability to bring business and industry experts into its programmes of mentorship for the micro-entrepreneurs. This "beyond the financing" strategy provides the requisite competencies to the micro-entrepreneurs and enables sustainability to their ventures. For a country as large as India, there is potential for many more NPOs organized on the model of BYST to support nano and micro enterprises.

(d) Microfinance corporation model
The Grameen Bank was founded by Muhammad Yunus in 1983 in Bangla Desh to provide tiny loans for the poor to enable self-employment. The success of the Grameen

Bank and the global recognition it secured is reflective of the potential of directed micro credit. Over a period of 26 years, the Bank created over 7.8 million active borrowers (cumulative) disbursing over USD 3.5 billion in tiny loans. The pioneering work in employment generation touching the lives of the poorest of the poor fetched for Yunus and the Grameen Bank the Nobel Peace Prize in 2006. Today the Grameen Bank has become more diversified in its product offerings, leading to greater generation of wealth for its customers. In India, microfinance sector took root very quickly over the last two decades, and some of them even received small bank licenses under the new regulations of the Reserve Bank of India.

Extending the concept further, but only recently under the new NDA Government led by Prime Minister Narendra Modi, a new bank called Micro Units Development and Refinance Agency (called MUDRA Bank) was established for development of micro units and refinance of MFIs to encourage entrepreneurship in a focused manner. This initiative can lead to creation of millions of micro enterprises in India. Potentially, MUDRA Bank and Small Industries Development Bank of India (SIDBI) and Regional Rural Banks (RRBs) can lead to establishment and scaling up of entrepreneurial enterprises, with a new financial energy. While rural banks did get set up in India even decades ago, their inability to lead an entrepreneurial revolution is related to adoption of policy driven mores of big banks rather than entrepreneurial risk taking approaches appropriate for microfinance. The new format and approach for microfinance corporations needs to be expanded in India.

(e) The Murthy-Catamaran model

The Catamaran Venture Capital fund was set up by Infosys founder, NR Narayana Murthy and his wife Sudha Murthy by selling their shares constituting a small part of their shareholding in Infosys to raise Rs 6 billion (USD 133 million). This amounted to 0.43 percent of the total capital of Infosys. The move by Narayana Murthy is a trend setter for successful entrepreneurs to share their wealth and expertise to reinvest in others' entrepreneurial ideas and create wealth for others and the society. The companies listed in the National Stock Exchange of India have a combined market capitalization of over USD 1 trillion. A sale of even 0.5 percent of the capital could lead to a massive USD 5 billion fund that could be set up to several Catamaran style venture capital funds.

Assuming that promoters of various listed companies own on average over 25 percent of the overall capital structure (and market capitalization), successful entrepreneur-heads of Indian corporations have in their hands a huge funding potential to support millions of micro, small and medium scale entrepreneurial enterprises. It would be stimulating if entrepreneur-heads of all listed companies, including public sector undertakings would dedicate at least 0.5 percent of their respective companies' shareholding/market capitalization to support entrepreneurial ventures. When this scale of finance is coupled with their personal commitment to mentor budding entrepreneurs a sea change would occur in the entrepreneurial scene. It is to be hoped that several other successful entrepreneurs as well as corporate group heads would replicate or improve upon the Catamaran model.

(f) Western venture capital model

Venture capital firms entered the Indian industrial scene in the 1990s in a big way along with the economic policy liberalization. Their entry was pursuant to a decision of the Government of India to allow foreign finance companies take stakes in the Indian companies. Taking small stakes of 10 to 25 percent in the capital structure of new as well as fast growing companies, venture capital firms enabled a number of first generation enterprises strengthen their equity structures and also list themselves on the bourses. Venture capital funds enable companies achieve the crucial leap from a modest beginning to a modern era, accessing technologies or markets through their financing. As companies are not typically listed at that stage, venture capital firms take stake based on stock pricing negotiated with the promoters. Seed funding and Series A, B and C funding constitute the primary support to start-ups.

While venture capital firms serve a valuable purpose their emphasis on growth and exit at attractive valuations, through listing or further sale to other strategic investors, tends to distort orderly growth of companies. Typically, venture capital firms help establish medium scale enterprises with their investments ranging between USD 10 to 50 million. Venture capital firms tend to be sector-savvy, betting on sunrise and entrepreneurially driven sectors. India's IT and pharmaceutical sectors in the 2000s benefitted from venture capital investments. Potentially, venture capital can support India's drive into sunrise sectors such as biotechnology, nanotechnology, healthcare, education, alternative fuels and clean technologies, providing confidence to entrepreneurs move into such sectors. That said, unless the Western venture capital funds tie up with Indian groups the ability to take risks relevant to the Indian scenario could be weak.

(g) Global private equity model

While venture capital and private equity funding is seen to be synonymous, private equity funds tend to favour listed companies for their investments. Most private equity firms enter established firms through preferential allotment of new shares to themselves at prices that reflect market valuations or reflect specific premiums based on their insights into business plans. While venture capital firms provide growth capital, private equity players provide funding for a variety of purposes including growth capital, capital for retiring debt, mezzanine funding and acquisition war chest. With investments that range from USD 50 to 200 million, private equity firms can truly shape medium scale enterprises become large corporations. However, the global economic downturn of 2008 and 2009 saw the weak foundations of organized venture capital and private equity industries.

The established private equity industry has global investors. Their investments are subject to returns to their investors, some of them extremely large and powerful ones such as global pension funds. In good times, these private equity players are nation and sector agnostic, seek a diversified investment portfolio and display a penchant for globalization of their portfolio firms. In difficult times, however, they tend to be extremely cautious and withdrawn. It is time that Indian financial institutions, gratuity and pension funds, mutual funds and provident funds as well as large public and private sector groups created India's own private equity behemoths.

(h) State as super equity player

As large firms grow larger, many grow beyond the reach of even large private equity players. Large firms and private equity players manage the situation by creating subsidiaries for newer activities and channelling equity flows. In countries such as India where government owned public sector undertakings (PSUs) occupy commanding heights of the economy, the State has to assume the role of a super public equity player or venture capital player, with respect to the PSUs. Several corporations in infrastructure sector have emerged due to such public investments by the Government of India. These, in turn, have led to creation of new strengths in the economy, which the private sector or the overseas players would have considered to be either beyond their means or their risk profile.

While a school of thought questions the efficiency and appropriateness of a large PSU sector, there is no denying that but for such investments many mega corporations in oil, gas, refining, power, power equipment, locomotives and other investment intensive sectors would not have been established. The induction of new technologies and establishment of new industries with uncertain commercialization opportunities requires massive investments which only governments are willing to make. The Government of India's disinvestment plans could unlock easily USD 10 to 20 billion depending on the PSUs chosen for disinvestment and stake sale levels. Though the Government plans to dedicate the proceeds to social service programs it would be equally logical to channel at least 50 percent of the proceeds to setting up new entrepreneurial and start-up ventures in long gestation, high technology sunrise sectors, with PSU support. Such an approach would provide technological assurance and employment security to the nation. An alternative could be for the listed PSUs to issue additional shares at premium to strategic investors and initiate such new generation enterprises.

(i) Government policy liberalization

Indian Government has helped the growth of medium and large scale sector by the dramatic policies of economic liberalization initiated in 1992. Further liberalization, however, happened only in steps and with certain periodicity. The NDA Government's thrust on diversified industrial development through Make in India, Start Up and Stand Up themes as well as the recent liberalization of foreign direct investment in hitherto guarded sectors such as aviation, defence equipment, brownfield pharmaceuticals and single brand retail should work to support high capacity entrepreneurial investment by Indian and foreign corporations. Liberalization policies, under execution as well as new ones, must have explicit linkages with indigenous entrepreneurial and start-up development.

The new Companies Act 2013 was expected to give a fillip to entrepreneurial activity with the One Person Company (OPC) provisions. This laudable reform in company law has, however, not resulted in the desired boost to entrepreneurial activity because of the revenue cap. Further, OPCs are ideal in supporting social infrastructure such as education, transportation and healthcare which are still rigidly governed by bureaucratic barriers to entry. Much of the liberalization responsibility in this sphere rests on the State Governments as well. The governments need to establish single windows to facilitate setting up of OPCs in a host of fields. The objectives of ensuring quality and safety are better served by establishing technology bodies to supervise quality and safety rather than by controlling entry.

Summary

Entrepreneurial energy can take shape in terms of entities with highly variable scale and scope. From nano to mega, enterprises can be positioned and grown depending on the applicable product-market scope in each case. As discussed in this chapter, India has as many as nine financing options with awesome financial power in the aggregate which can be made available to finance varied types of entrepreneurial ventures under different modes. Profitable firms and successful investors can raise money by selling a small portion of their holdings periodically to set up and expand venture capital entities which will offer not only finance but also mentorship by the successful entrepreneurs and corporate leaders. The Governments, Central and State, can also play catalytic roles in promoting such financial options for entrepreneurial ventures in different capacities.

The financing models of not-for-profit and microfinance corporations have demonstrated how focus and reach can create a viable start-up network. At the other points of spectrum established venture capital funds and private equity players have to rework their models and become more entrepreneurial by themselves. Indian mutual funds, pension funds and provident fund organizations as well as corporate groups have to set up India's own venture capital and private sector funds. At the apex level the Government has to rediscover its role as a super venture capital investor, gaining additional financial capability from the envisaged PSU disinvestment program. Financial entrepreneurship has to be seen as the trigger for emergence of a full spectrum of nano, micro, small, medium, large and mega entrepreneurial entities in India.

CHAPTER 13

National Start-up Models

From Start-up to Maturity: Indian Entrepreneurial Challenge

Indian psyche is unique in that it follows an icon as much as it chooses independence. Indian corporate saga is an equally unique amalgam of followership and independence. The growth of Indian enterprise is founded on an entrepreneurial rush into an activity that is opened up. The evolution of industrial structure in India is based on a continuous expansion in the number of firms in the fray rather than a structural consolidation at any point of time. The Indian corporate sector therefore faces a challenge as firms struggle to transform themselves from start-up stage to maturity state, some passing successfully through a growth phase, and some failing to. The challenge, if left unaddressed, could affect entrepreneurial development, and eventually the competitiveness of the Indian corporate sector.

The Indian Industrial Evolution

The Indian industrial start-up model, as elsewhere, was fuelled by entrepreneurial energy. Even when India was under foreign occupation, in the 1800s and the early 1900s, Indian industrial start-ups were established by the Tatas and Birlas, with their enterprises becoming large industrial groups over the decades. Post-independence, successive government policies enabled and encouraged establishment of scores of cottage and small scale enterprises in India. Some of these served larger firms as suppliers and vendors of materials and components while several other start-ups sought a direct go-to-market strategy, with varying degrees of success.

An introverted India, even post-independence in 1947, rarely encouraged free entry and exit, expansion of scale and induction of technology in its industrial and economic policies. As a result, companies stagnated and became less competitive, relative to global trends. At the same time, licensing regulations inhibited global corporations from entering into or expanding in India. On a helpful side, process patent policies (as in some other countries) ensured freedom for domestic companies to reverse-engineer global products for Indian markets. The Indian automobile and pharmaceutical industries became, for example, the epitome of low-scale, domestic-oriented fragmented industrial structures of the 1960s and 1970s.

There emerged a new Indian entrepreneurial wave from the 1970s (Ambani founded Reliance, for example). Technology induction and assimilation blazed new paths from the 1980s (Indo-Japanese automobile collaborations such as Maruti-Suzuki). Entrepreneurs and corporations were freed from the excessive controls, and certain industries started becoming global leaders in certain sectors from the 1990s (TCS and Infosys, in Information Technology, for example). Increasing confidence in Indian competencies and policies from the 2000s and post-patent harmonization assurances led to greater global interest in India with a better awareness of the competitiveness of Indian enterprise. Simultaneously, Indian industrial groups and larger Indian companies became globally aggressive, entering overseas markets (directly and through partnerships), acquiring overseas units and marquee brands.

The Indian Start-up Model

From a highly protected and regulated domestic regime that existed till 1992, the industrial paradigm in India evolved into a liberalized, competitive globalized regime through the 1990s and in the 2000s. The base models that helped Indian start-ups to enter and stay fixed in scale and scope are, however, becoming less tenable. The Indian start-ups are today verily at cross roads, with choices between smug stagnation and tough transformation. Yet, the continued proliferation of owner-managed companies and small scale enterprises with dated technologies indicates that a new start-up model is yet to emerge.

The Indian start-up model is highly domestic market oriented and self-reliance inspired. The original model focused on just being suppliers to big companies and to their tier 1 suppliers. This scenario is changing now. While start-up firms would not be averse to being suppliers to larger firms, especially in sectors such as engineering and automobile, the overwhelming preference seems to be on direct go-to-market strategies. This enables firms have a quick market-oriented entry in any industrial segment but also limits the ability of entrepreneurs to create stable, growth or niche models that could be more vibrant technologically and commercially in the long term.

The missing dimensions in the Indian start-up scenario relate to inadequate access to technology, insufficient financial resources and overwhelming reluctance to consolidate. The first two factors dictate the pace with which a start-up in India is able to navigate to, and through, the growth phase while the last factor dictates the ability of a start-up firm to stay on course in the growth phase or navigate the maturity phase. Typically, a start-up in India would have the capability to grow from an annual sales level of USD 1 million to USD 100 million but lack the capability to move beyond without dedicated efforts to manage the three dimensions of technology, finance and ownership.

An examination of the Western and Japanese models of start-up could provide guidance for new development models relevant for Indian start-ups.

The Western and Japanese Start-up Models

The Western and Japanese start-up models are typically based on pioneering pieces of technology or market creation. While it may be tempting to relate this to the fact that all modern technologies emanated in the West (largely USA or Europe) or in Japan it is the start-up intent that made the difference. Entrepreneurs with truly ground-breaking products in the West or in Japan or Korea went on to make their start-ups into mega global enterprises. However, there are certain typical nuances of technology-led start-up development that are different.

Not all techno-entrepreneurs in the West were, or are, keen to build their start-up enterprises into mega enterprises. Entrepreneurs in the West see technology as a concept to be commercially proved as products or services at their hands rather than necessarily as scaled up businesses in their hands. They also see creation of commercial value (for themselves) as more important than either staying in the market or expanding the scale of the enterprise. Finally, entrepreneurs are willing to monetize their technologies and firms to generate surpluses for new endeavours. Philosophically, ownership and management are treated as very important in the start-up phase but are considered expendable for leading into the growth and maturity phases. In this approach, entrepreneurs benefit from an equity environment that provides multiple-series funding.

The techno-entrepreneurs in Japan are different. They tend to innovate for larger industrial firms or trading groups and in the process help create multi-level business arrangements. The start-ups established by the techno-entrepreneurs typically grow with the larger firms and groups, and become global enterprises in their own right. The entrepreneurs are typically committed to their technologies and attached to their groups but are also able to evolve to the higher levels due to a positive synergy from parent and supplier relationships. Typically, the larger firms in Japan respect the origins and independence of the smaller suppliers and desist from the Western temptation of acquiring promising technologies and firms. Instead, the accent is on letting the smaller start-ups grow into mature, innovative enterprises.

A Hybrid Model for Indian Start-ups

Given the constraints the Indian start-ups face in accessing technology, finance and markets, and the attachment of the entrepreneurs to continued ownership of the firms they founded, a hybrid model is relevant for Indian start-ups. Assuming that a base level of promoter and external funding is arranged, typically, start-ups fall into one of the three categories: those that make better use of available technology, those that make their operations more competitive and those that access certain market segments more creatively. Needless to say, firms which achieve a virtuous combination of technological innovation, operational efficiency and market penetration would be in a position to drive into a growth phase on their own. The hybrid model would be relevant to start-ups having competencies in one of the three dimensions.

Firms which are technologically innovative need to aim at achieving the earliest proof of concept, following which they should be prepared to license or sell the technology to larger firms which can take the product to the market. This phenomenon is widely prevalent in the West, especially in technology and biopharmaceutical fields, and needs to be adapted to the Indian situation. Firms which have pieces of market would do well by either taking in products from other start-ups or providing market access to larger firms. Firms which are operationally efficient must focus on gaining market access in partnership with larger firms having Indian and global market presence. This could enable a longer independent functioning to such firms, enabling growth journey on their own.

The hybrid model for Indian start-ups thus envisages growth through inorganic relationships across fragments of value chain rather than through organic end-to-end value chain. Many Indian start-ups in India have evolved into mid-sized firms through such inorganic relationships. Still some decisions have to be customized: for example, the scale and scope of such relationships, whether such relationships would need to be limited period relationships or permanent relationships, and whether the end game is surplus generation through value monetization and exit as per the Western model or lifetime domain commitment as per the Asian model.

Founder-Manager Transformational Issues

Part of the evolutionary response would emerge from how the founders of the Indian start-ups manage the entry, growth and maturity phases of an enterprise. Entrepreneurial firms tend to be typically founder managed. Investors gain confidence with the founder being in total control of the enterprise while the employees get inspired by the leadership of their founder. As enterprises move into growth phases, investors need to let go of their control on the founders, and the founders need to let go of their control on their enterprises. As an enterprise becomes larger it needs to organize itself into organizational and business units that can be driven by independent managers to generate greater value.

While no professional manager can bring the passion and feel of a founder-leader to an enterprise, start-ups need to find ways and means of institutionalizing the entrepreneurial passion and feel through diversified professionalization. Indian start-ups which moved into the big league have done so not only on the basis of 'technology-efficiency-market' model but also due to organizational development. Serial entrepreneurship could well help Indian entrepreneurs to continue to feel their passion with newer enterprises while enabling their earlier enterprises move on their own steam.

The suggested organizational model is based on the unique Indian psyche that complies as much as it commands; that follows as much as it leads; and that is as much professional as it is entrepreneurial. Compensating any limitations it has, the Indian employee base is driven by a deep sense of loyalty and frugality that can be leveraged by placing capable people in commanding positions. The success of large Indian private and public sector corporations is related to the diversified ownership model that is extended to individual organizational units of an enterprise.

Science and Finance for Start-up Transformation

Start-ups need access to science and technology. Indian entrepreneurs are adept at adapting technology, enhancing efficiency and perching their firms on market niches. They are, however, diffident in taking science and technology from Indian research laboratories. For example, there are over 40 specialized laboratories under the umbrella of the Council for Scientific and Industrial Research (CSIR) which is one of the largest publicly funded research networks in the world. In addition, institutes of higher learning such as Indian Institutes of Technology and Indian Institute of Science have cutting edge researchers. These competencies can be leveraged to establish new drivers of growth through win-win commercial arrangements. Indian start-ups can place just a small proportion of the risk on using and developing indigenous science and technology to secure cost-effective business development. There is a great potential for Indian science and technology that is waiting to be captured.

Western and Japanese angel investors and private equity funds can achieve substantial returns by considering multi-phase investments in Indian start-ups that could transform themselves into future growth engines by utilizing India specific science and technology. Softbank has been a leader in this approach. There must, however, be more opportunities and platforms for interactions between such investors and the Indian start-ups. There is tremendous potential that is untapped in social and industrial infrastructure, as well as rural and urban development. A comparative inventory of small enterprises in US, Europe and Japan with those existing in India indicates the enormous possibilities.

Central and State Governments in India have traditionally supported start-ups by policy measures. Newer and more creative measures are required. Encouragement of One Person Companies, creation of financial exchanges exclusively for start-ups, enablement of crowdfunding mechanisms, freedom to accept advances and deposits, channelling of a certain proportion of CSIR research effort for small enterprises, creation of start-up finance divisions in all banks and financial institutions, small bank licenses exclusively for start-ups, more aggressive capitalization of MUDRA Bank, creation of a fund-of-funds for start-ups, exemption of small enterprise promotion and management from complex legal, regulatory and registration processes (and hurdles) and encouragement of mentoring of start-ups by working executives, all of these supported by governmental policies, could add up to a great entrepreneurial start-up movement in India.

CHAPTER 14

Entrepreneurial Ecosystems

"Too Big to Fail" versus "Too Small to Grow": A Few Perspectives from the Indian and Japanese Micro Business Ecosystems

Indian business and industrial ecosystem has had, until recently, no exit or bankruptcy provisions as in the US. The Indian Parliament has passed in May 2016 the Insolvency and Bankruptcy Code 2016 but execution would remain the key. In fact, Indian business ventures are traditionally expected to be resilient in adversities and aggressive with opportunities. Like the oriental philosophy, the spirit of the enterprise is expected to linger on for perpetuity. This is rightly so as India needs to be on a virtuous cycle of continued growth and employment in its quest to reach its full potential. With resources being scarce, both the completely capitalistic view (survival of the fittest) and the completely *laissez faire* view (the markets will eventually correct) are perhaps not so appropriate for the Indian economy at this stage.

That said, failure (which starts with loss of competitiveness, and ends with close of operations) is also an inevitable consequence of a globalized economy and fragmented industry structure. While there have been stories the world over of failures being turned around into successes, the preferable option is not to fail at all. In this context, the declaration by the Indian Union Government of two of the largest banks in India, the State Bank of India (SBI) and the ICICI Bank, as being "too big to fail" comes as a fresh thought, probably taking off from the viewpoints that emerged after the 2008 global financial crisis. The markets, however, did not seem impressed. The declaration possibly needed to be backed up with concrete initiatives to achieve strong profiles (such as SBI merging its five associate banks and Bharatiya Mahila Bank with itself). Also required is an approach to remedy the constraints that keep small scale firms too small to grow.

Big may be Bountiful, but...

In developed economic ecosystems, big is considered bountiful. Size is considered to bring advantages of economies of scale and scope, providing several levers for driving business competitiveness. Growth, however, is a function of time and effort. It is also a function of adjacency of several related businesses. If one looks at the Indian automobile industry, there is clearly a difference between the bigness of a company like Tata Motors which manufactures virtually every type of four wheeler (car, utility vehicle, commercial vehicle) versus the bigness of Maruti Suzuki which specializes only in passenger cars. Similar examples of specialized scale versus diversified scale can be found across industries. There is no set theory on when and how adjacencies must be actively sought out to achieve bigness or, on the contrary, when and how they turn out to be disincentives for growth.

The aspiration for bigness as an end in itself is a deeply ingrained characteristic of human behaviour. Bigness is taken as the marker for achievement. Listings of the largest firms by leading business magazines such as Fortune and Forbes abroad or Business Today or Business India in India have only positioned the concept of big being praiseworthy in an unassailable way. Bigness has negative consequences for the firms, industries and economies too. Apart from vulnerability to smaller and nimble competitors, in economically adverse situations they are sharply impacted. As an example, a free fall in oil prices (imagine a deep slump from USD 100 to USD 20 per barrel), oil exploration firms are not only roiled for short term performance but also forced to drastically prune investments for the long term. Steel giants in India that have grown with huge reliance on debt are negatively impacted by the decline in global steel demand and pricing. As long as bigness is accompanied by deep cash, the advantage of being big sustains through the crises.

Small is Essential

Big may be bountiful for developed countries but for emerging economies like India small is still critical. India can be considered to be a pioneer in encouraging setting up of small scale enterprises, from the early days of independence. In fact, the emphasis on cottage industries was a well merited approach towards sustaining and developing rural artisanship, individual craftsmanship and distributed self-employment. The reason for the lukewarm impact of this pioneering effort can be attributed to ignorance of the need for, and challenges of, integrating high technology with low scale in the small scale sector. Reverting to the case of automotive industry or aerospace industry, nuts, bolts and washers or springs could be simple to make but need complex technology for quality and endurance, which in turn calls for major investments.

There are areas where technology, in recent years, has helped small enterprises in marketing, and to an extent even in design. However, manufacturing continues to present major challenges for integration of high technology and small scale. India's success in Make in India theme would depend on how this complex challenge is tackled. India's new start-up economy is highly encouraging but given its preponderant orientation towards services and information technology, it hardly offers a solution for the small scale industry's manufacturing owes and resource constraints. High technology equipment and new generation materials require investments which the small scale sector can ill afford while skilled scientists and engineers are not easily attracted to small enterprises. Low entry barriers to setting up of manufacturing enterprises in small scale in India only compounds the difficulties.

Big for Small

India needs a different paradigm. Angel funding rushes to sectors and firms where it anticipates huge valuations or good returns. It is unlikely to venture into areas of manufacturing which require high investments for high technologies on one hand but are driven down by low margins of supplies to big customers who have immense bargaining power on the other. Big customers would need to take a broader perspective on this front, in the context of what could impact their income statements vis-à-vis balance sheets. In short, they would need to set up a venture capital pool to support small scale manufacturing enterprises. In a sense, it could be a revert to the early days of industrialization when big companies, mostly public sector units, set up their exclusive ancillary estates to enable contiguous, parent-supported manufacture.

Such exclusivity has, over the years, been eroded by the desire of small and medium units to seek wider markets even as big firms started feeling the responsibility of nurturing units as being uneconomical. The concept of big units sponsoring the smaller ones, however, continues to be relevant. Industrial parks which house the parent corporation and ancillary units is a common feature in modern India as well as developed countries. The challenge to corporations and such small units is how the smaller units on a growth path can be weaned away from the need for nurturing, and how new small units can come into play independent of such sponsorship. The earlier Small Industries Development Bank of India (SIDBI) and the new Micro Units Development and Refinance Agency (MUDRA) Bank are evidences that the Indian governments are well aware of the need to support the small scale and micro sectors. The need, however, is for a more intensive and a more cohesive effort as in Japan.

Japan's SME Ecosystem

For people used to seeing only the big Japanese brands, it would be a revelation that small and medium enterprises account for 99.7 percent of all firms, over 70 percent of employment and more than 50 percent of all value added in the manufacturing industry. Japan's industrial policy under SME Basic Act viewed SMEs, including micro units, as diverse, dynamic and independent drivers of manufacturing industry. The Japanese Government promulgated a host of acts and set up several agencies including an exclusive university system, a dedicated financial corporation and credit reinsurance support for SMEs. The policy, which also provides for lower income tax rates, recognized that SMEs have weak assets and lack access to finance as well as human resources and established a total SME ecosystem under the control of Ministry of Economy, Trade and Industry (METI). Annual budgets provide for significant financial support to

SMEs. Large units also enrich the SME ecosystem through technological support, deputation of retired personnel as mentors and acceptance of single-sourcing. They realize that the hidden strength of their component makers underpins their own end-product quality.

While India may have the structures and processes, lack of adequate and focused budgetary support as well as necessary credit enhancement and credit reinsurance schemes for entrepreneurial and start-up ventures is a lacuna. More importantly, Japan SME policy succeeds because of the uniquely Japanese obsession with technology and quality as well as development of human resources. A great example is the project to upgrade strategic core technologies to support automobile and engineering industries. Under this, 22 specific core manufacturing fields were identified to upgrade technologies and processes through experimental research and commercialization. As a result, and as an example, precision forging replaced raw forging plus machining for select automobile parts, saving costs and improving quality. In consumer products, ceramic and pottery industry collaborated with fountain pen industry to develop highly precise and elegant porcelain fountain pens.

As part of improving access to skilled human resources for SME sector, 9 universities were set up in Japan exclusively for SMEs. Trade and business organizations to support start-ups and enable overseas business expansion were also set up. While India may have such initiatives in some measure or the other, what differentiates the Japanese SME ecosystem is the integrated governmental approach which not only conceptualizes programmes and provides budgetary support but also monitors and counsels SME sector in terms of specific technology and business deliverables. Indian Governments and Industries would do well to study the Japanese SME ecosystem and transfer relevant paradigms that could transform the Indian SME and Micro sector from the image of low cost and low quality to one of high technology and competitive cost with access to State-funded and private-participated credit enhancement and skill honing institutions.

EPILOGUE

Entrepreneurial Thermodynamics

Passionate Entrepreneurship: Defying the Laws of Thermodynamics?

Although entrepreneurship is seen largely as an organizational or behavioural phenomenon, the challenges and paradoxes of sustainable entrepreneurship can be better understood in a thermodynamic perspective. All things in the observable universe are affected by and obey the laws of thermodynamics. Entrepreneurial systems are no exception. If entrepreneurial energy is considered the heat of a heat engine, the laws of thermodynamics apply strikingly to systems analysis of entrepreneurship. Entrepreneurial energy provides the power to performance of a start-up firm. Just as temperature, pressure and chemical potential of a heat system dictate the thermodynamic behaviour of a heat engine, energy, passion and competencies of an entrepreneurial system dictate its behaviour.

Organizational Entropy

As an analogous concept, entropy is a thermodynamic property that is a measure of the energy not available for useful work in a thermodynamic process such as in energy conversion devices, engines, or machines. Such devices can only be driven by convertible energy, and have a theoretical maximum efficiency when converting energy to work. During this work entropy accumulates in the system, but has to be removed by dissipation in the form of waste heat. Many entrepreneurial systems are affected by the entropy caused by the lag that typically exists between the passionate fast-forward of the entrepreneur and the conservative status quo of his leadership and managerial team.

About the Author and Publisher

Dr C Bhaktavatsala Rao holds a Ph.D. Degree in Industrial Management and an M. Tech. Degree in Industrial Engineering, both from the Indian Institute of Technology, Madras, Chennai, and a B.E. Degree in Mechanical Engineering from Sri Venkateswara University, Tirupati.

Dr CB Rao has forty-two years of diversified experience in strategic and operational leadership of large reputed companies, including global MNCs, in India.

Dr CB Rao has led the companies he was associated with on paths of rapid growth and value creation. A business leader with deep roots in pharmaceutical and automobile industries, with a strong grasp over all functional domains, he has undertaken several growth-driving and value-building integration and diversification initiatives for the companies he was associated with. He is a prolific writer with over 130 publications in economic and business dailies and refereed journals to his credit. He runs his management blog under the name Strategy Musings at cbrao2008.blogspot.com where he posts articles on different aspects of strategy and leadership regularly.

Leadercrest Academy is established by Dr CB Rao to leverage his knowledge and experience, in collaboration with other experts, as a world class institution for leadership development, competitive strategy and corporate governance that would enable business and industrial excellence. Leadercrest is committed, among others, to publish books and reading materials to support its objectives.

www.ingramcontent.com/pod-product-compliance
Lightning Source LLC
Chambersburg PA
CBHW031414210526
45464CB00005B/1875

Laws of Thermodynamics

The postulate that an entrepreneur is one who creates something out of nothing, evidently challenges the first law of thermodynamics, which is an expression of the principle of conservation of energy. The law expresses that energy can be transformed, i.e. changed from one form to another, but can neither be created nor be destroyed. It is usually formulated by stating that the change in the internal energy of the system is equal to the amount of heat supplied to the system, minus the amount of work performed by the system on its surroundings. However, to the extent that a successful entrepreneur draws more than proportionate output from lean inputs, whether meagre financial resources, insufficient talent pool, indifferent regulatory policies or inadequate market perception, a true entrepreneur challenges the first law of thermodynamics. Drawing lessons from this, however, entrepreneurship in India would fly even higher if (i) financing options for entrepreneurial firms are expanded substantially, (ii) talented people opt enthusiastically to support entrepreneurs, (iii) regulatory agencies provide fast-track single window support to start-ups and expansion projects, and (iv) customers encourage indigenous entrepreneurial product and service offerings. These are also sources of additional energy for the Indian entrepreneurial system.

No two entrepreneur systems can be alike. This is because no firm, much less an entrepreneurial system, is insulated from the external ecosystem (as in a thermodynamic adiabatic process). Adiabatic processes of thermodynamics between two specified states of a closed system specify that the net work done is the same regardless of the nature of the closed system and the details of the process. Entrepreneurs who refuse to be insulated and introverted and, in contrast, excel in interacting with the eco system as well as in influencing to achieve positive outcomes achieve superior results. Successful entrepreneurs need to be seen, felt and experienced by various stakeholders, from employees to investors, from domestic associates to international partners, and from local governments to central government to reinforce faith in entrepreneurial capabilities. Entrepreneurs have to be sensitive to external ecosystems to manage their expectations in a non-adiabatic fashion.

Systems of entrepreneurial energy calibrate with the second law of thermodynamics as well. The second law of thermodynamics is an expression of the tendency that over time, differences in temperature, pressure, and chemical potential equilibrate in an isolated physical system. From the state of thermodynamic equilibrium, the law deduces the principle of the increase of entropy and explains the phenomenon of irreversibility in nature. The second law of thermodynamics, also known as the law of increased entropy postulates the loss of matter and energy gradually over time. Usable energy of a power system is used for productivity, growth and repair. In the process, usable energy is converted into unusable energy. Thus, usable energy is irretrievably lost in the form of unusable energy. The greater the unusable energy the greater would be the inefficiency of the system. Entropy is defined, in practical thermodynamics, as a measure of unusable energy within a closed or isolated system (even, the universe as the ultimate example). As usable energy decreases and unusable energy increases, "entropy" increases. Entropy is also a gauge of randomness or chaos within a closed system. As usable energy is irretrievably lost, disorganization, randomness and chaos increase.

The second law of thermodynamics has several lessons for entrepreneurial organizations. Just as no heat engine is one hundred percent efficient, no entrepreneurial engine is totally efficient. It would be inappropriate on the part of entrepreneurs to expect their organizational energy levels to match their individual entrepreneurial energy levels. Smart and practical entrepreneurs, therefore, accept the theory of entropy and work towards minimizing the heat loss rather than expect the organizations to outperform their own energy levels. The second law implies that heat can never move from a colder body to a hotter body. So is it in entrepreneurial organizations; organizational teams would sap the energy of an entrepreneur unless the teams themselves are made up of high energy, entrepreneurial members. The need to look beyond the founder's capabilities and build a high performance team, preferably also an entrepreneurial one too, is evident for the long term sustainability of entrepreneurial organizations.

The third law of thermodynamics, though much less known relative to the other two laws, is equally important for entrepreneurial organizations. It states that the entropy of a heat system attains zero when the system reaches the absolute zero temperature (Kelvin temperature of minus 273 degrees centigrade). The third law of thermodynamics means that as the temperature of a system approaches absolute zero, its entropy approaches a constant (for pure perfect crystals, this constant is zero). A pure perfect crystal is one in which every molecule is identical, and the molecular alignment is perfectly even throughout the substance. For non-pure crystals, or those with less-than perfect alignment, there will be some energy associated with the imperfections, so the entropy cannot become zero. Drawing an analogy, if an entrepreneurial organization becomes a pure perfect crystal organization, ie., an organization in which each employee has at least the same energy and talent level as the founder-entrepreneur then the entropy or loss in the system would become zero. As we can appreciate, such a pure perfect crystal organization is an impossibility. Entrepreneurs would do well, however, to seek high energy levels within their organizations to the best extent possible, providing opportunities of empowerment and business building to such members. Otherwise, as with Google and other entrepreneurial organizations, high entrepreneurial energy individuals would migrate to establish their own ventures.

Minimizing Entropy and Maximizing Energy Usage

The laws of thermodynamics are absolute physical laws - everything in the observable universe is subject to them. Like time or gravity, nothing in the universe is exempt from these laws. Human and corporate entrepreneurial systems are no exception. The laws of thermodynamics, the law of energy conservation, the law of energy loss and the law of zero entropy, urge the entrepreneurs to look beyond themselves and model their organizations around the core concept of entrepreneurial energy. Neither egoistic defiance nor fatal compliance to the entrepreneurial thermodynamics would ensure sustainability of entrepreneurial energy. Institutionalization of entrepreneurial energy through structure and talent optimizes entrepreneurial thermodynamics.